A Siddur for Families and Schools

Michelle Shapiro Abraham, Editor

Readings and Translations
by Michelle Shapiro Abraham

Art by Katie Lipsitt

Central Conference of American Rabbis
5773 New York 2013

Michelle Shapiro Abraham, Editor
Readings and Translations by Michelle Abraham Shapiro
Art by Katie Lipsitt

Rabbi Hara E. Person, Publisher, CCAR Press

Rabbi Steven A. Fox, Chief Executive,
Central Conference of American Rabbis

Youth Siddur Advisory Group
Rabbi Paula Feldstein, Chair

Rabbi Deborah Bodin Cohen	Rabbi Joui M. Hessel, RJE	Rabbi Maurice A Salth
Rabbi Melissa Buyer, RJE	Rabbi Daniel Plotkin	Rabbi Cory Weiss
Rabbi Sharon G. Forman	Rabbi Steven H. Rau, RJE	Rabbinic Student Joshua Beraha
Rabbi Nicole Greninger		Rabbinic Student Daniel Kirzane

Library of Congress Cataloging-in-Publication Data

Mishkan t'filah for children : a Siddur for families and schools / Michelle Shapiro Abraham, editor ; readings and translations by Michelle Shapiro Abraham ; art by Katie Lipsitt.
   pages cm
ISBN 978-0-88123-201-1 (hardcover; Hebrew opening : alk. paper)
1. Siddurim—Texts—Juvenile literature. 2. Reform Judaism—Liturgy—Texts—Juvenile literature. I. Abraham, Michelle Shapiro, editor of compilation, translator, writer of added commentary. II. Lipsitt, Katie, illustrator. III. Central Conference of American Rabbis. IV. Siddur (Reform). English. Selections. V. Siddur (Reform). Hebrew. Selections.
BM674.36.A272 2013
296.4'5046083—dc23
                              2013013342

Copyright © 2013 Central Conference of American Rabbis.
Printed in U.S.A. All rights reserved. No portion of this book may be copied in any form for any purpose without written permission of the Central Conference of American Rabbis.

17 16 15 14 13 12 6 5 4 3 2

CCAR Press, 355 Lexington Avenue, New York, NY 10017
(212) 972-3636
www.ccarpress.org

In memory of
Rabbi Richard Saul Sternberger
who loved children.

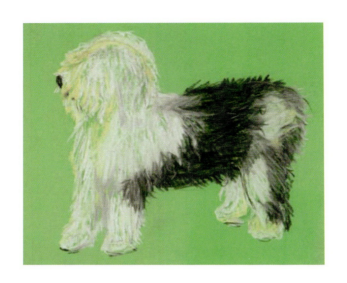

How to Use This Siddur

Mishkan T'filah for Children is designed to not only introduce young children to the structure and order of the prayer service, but also to help them develop their own kavanah—intentionality—when praying. Using poems, readings, and images, *Mishkan T'filah for Children* strives to create a holy space for children and their families to experience the wonder of God and the power of communal worship together.

Our rabbis knew that each of us experiences God differently, and so they embedded in our worship service different views and images of the Divine. In *Mishkan T'filah for Children* we have tried to keep this varied view of God in the creative translations, prayers and writings. By using capital letters as hints that we are calling God by name, *Mishkan T'filah* draws on the both traditional and modern images, calling God "Artist," "Ruler," "Love," and "Holy Spark." In this way, we hope to remind our students that there are many ways to view God in the Jewish tradition, and that the prayerbook gives us an opportunity to "try out" these different images and explore what is meaningful to us.

Chatimot

One of the unique features of *Mishkan T'filah* is the use of *chatimot*, the signature lines of a prayer. In *Mishkan T'filah*, the *chatimah* is used at the bottom of the prayer on the right facing page, and again under the alternative interpretation or poem used on the facing left page. In this way, whether you use the material on the right or the left, you are able to conclude with the same signature phrase. *Mishkan T'filah for Children* follows this same paradigm, repeating the *chatimah* on both the right and left facing pages, even when the version of the prayer on the left page is visual and not textual.

In addition, both under the pictures and at the end of prayers, we have chosen to maintain the Hebrew phrase *"Baruch atah, Adonai"* in the translation, thus exposing early readers to the repeating prayer formula and bringing them in to the words of our tradition.

Art

Art, as we know, is a powerful tool. As the adage states, "a picture is worth a thousand words." This is indeed the case for young children. I see the images in this prayerbook as visual prayers. When leading the service, consider asking your community how the picture makes them feel, or simply have them sit for a moment and consider the artistic interpretation of the prayer. Then, join in the chatimah together at the bottom of the picture, showing young students that pondering a piece of art can indeed be a prayer of the heart.

Organization and Graphics

Even young children can understand that a prayerbook has an order with sections and specific prayers. Using graphic elements such as color and images to organize this siddur, young children can learn these different sections and build a strong foundation for a lifetime of worship participation. With the help of these graphics, we have included both morning and evening services for Shabbat and weekdays in *Mishkan T'filah for Children*. For an evening service, simply follow the moon icon through the book ☾, and for a morning service, simply follow the sun icon ☀.

Which Services Are Included In This Siddur

The first service in this siddur is a Shabbat service. It includes both evening and morning services. The moon and sun icons indicate whether that page is for evening or morning.

The second service in this siddur is a weekday service. It too includes both evening and morning services. Again, the moon and sun icons indicate whether that page is for evening or morning.

The siddur contains one Torah reading section, and one section of concluding prayers.

When to Use This Siddur

Mishkan T'filah for Children is designed for family services and school worship services. The first service is meant to used primarily for family services, and the second service is meant to be used primarily in a school setting, but there is no reason you can't use it as you see fit. In addition, it is also meant to be used as a companion for young readers in "regular" services. Consider having *Mishkan T'filah for Children* out for young children at your regular Shabbat evening or morning service. While parents are praying from *Mishkan T'filah*, children can follow along (by following the "sun" or "moon") with the pictures and words found in *Mishkan T'filah for Children*.

Each community is unique, and therefore we have left the last few pages of this siddur blank. We have done this so that your community can add their own songs and prayers, personalizing the siddur to your own needs and your own worship style. We have also chosen not to include songs within the body of the siddur itself, recognizing that musical choices vary greatly from synagogue to synagogue.

May *Mishkan T'filah for Children* help create a holy space for you and the children of your community, as you join together in worship, song and celebration together.

Acknowledgments

Many thanks my 2012 URJ Eisner Camp Faculty Chevre who sat with me in the Kivie Kaplan Center sharing ideas, comments, laughter and support while I crafted the words of this siddur: Rabbi Todd Markley, Michele Markley, Rabbi Joel Abraham, Rabbi David Levy, Beth Kramer Mazer, Cantor Gail Hirschenfang, Rabbi Danny Polish, Rabbi Peter Stein, and Rabbi Jonathan Hecht.

Thank you to Rabbi Hara Person who led and guided this process, and Rabbi Paula Feldstein, the chair of the Youth Siddur Advisory Group, who shared her wisdom. Thanks also go to rabbinic student Daniel Kirzane for his fine editorial work, CCAR staff members Debbie Smilow, Ortal Bensky, and Dan Medwin for supplying Hebrew texts and many other ways that they helped bring this book to fruition, as well as Rebecca Neimark, Debra Hirsch Corman, and Michelle Kwitkin-Close for all of their fine, caring work in their respective areas.

We are also very grateful to the members of the Worship and Practice Committee who reviewed and commented on the manuscript, including Rabbi Elaine Zecher (chair), Rabbi David Adelson, Rabbi Nicole M. Greninger, Rabbi Beth Schwartz, and Rabbi Joel Sisenwine.

A special thank you to my husband, Rabbi Joel Abraham, who challenged me to see the siddur of our tradition in a new way, and empowered me to look deeper for translations and interpretations that inspired me. Without his support, insights, and love, this prayer book would not be what you hold in your hands today.

A very special thank you goes to Sam Simon, Rabbi Laszlo Berkowits, and Rabbi Amy Schwartzman, who helped ensure that the memory of their dear friend Rabbi Richard Saul Sternberger would live on in this most fitting tribute to the values about which he cared deeply.

The children of Temple Sholom in Fanwood, NJ helped inspire this siddur. Your wonder, insights and joyful singing remind me each Shabbat of what a *k'hilah k'doshah*—a holy community—can be.

—Michelle Shapiro Abraham, RJE

Contents

Shabbat Evening and
Morning Service for Families

1

Reading of the Torah

56

Weekday Evening
and Morning Service

64

Concluding Prayers

106

שַׁבָּת עַרְבִית וְשַׁחֲרִית לְמִשְׁפָּחוֹת

**Shabbat Evening
and Morning Services
for Families**

Kabbalat Shabbat קַבָּלַת שַׁבָּת
Welcoming Shabbat

Sing a New Song

The little girl sat beside her grandfather in the service. Hebrew songs filled the room, but she didn't know a single one. She didn't know the Hebrew prayers or even the English ones. She wanted to join with everyone and pray to God. Very quietly, she began to sing to herself.

Each part of the prayer service was filled with blessings and dreams and hopes. She snuggled closer to her grandfather, twisting the strings of his tallit with her fingers. She wanted to join with everyone and pray to God. Moved by the service, and excited to hear her own voice, she began to sing a little louder.

The rabbi opened the splendid ark doors. Inside the ark was the Torah, with its beautiful covering and shiny breastplate. All the people stood. The little girl wanted to join everyone as they prayed to God. This time, she forgot to sing quietly. She began to sing out, as loudly as she could.

Everyone turned and stared at her. She snuggled up close to her grandfather, trying to hide in his tallit. The cantor walked off of the bimah. She knelt down beside the girl. "What you are singing?" she asked softly.

"It is my own song," the little girl said, her voice trembling. "I just wanted to pray to God." She looked at the floor and kicked her feet. "But I didn't know the words. I'm sorry." The cantor just smiled at her, a big, warm smile, and walked back onto the bimah.

The cantor turned to face the congregation. "In the Book of Psalms we are taught, 'Sing a new song unto God.' This morning, this little girl has sung a new song for us. She has reminded

קַבָּלַת שַׁבָּת
KABBALAT SHABBAT
WELCOMING SHABBAT

us that it is not the words of our mouths but the words of our heart that matter. She has sung her own song and in doing so has taught us all a new song to sing unto God." The cantor smiled again, and then, in her beautiful voice, she began to sing the little girl's song.

And everyone in the congregation joined in.

(Adapted from a Chasidic tale)

קַבָּלַת שַׁבָּת
KABBALAT SHABBAT
WELCOMING SHABBAT

Shirei Shabbat שִׁירֵי שַׁבָּת
Songs for Shabbat

Thank You, God

Baruch atah, Adonai, thank You, God.

Thank You for the candles,
Thank You for the wine,
Thank You for the challah
That always tastes so fine.

Baruch atah, Adonai, thank You, God.

Thank You for the mommies, thank You for dads,
They love us when we're happy,
They love us when we're sad.

Baruch atah, Adonai, thank You, God.

Bim Bam Shabbat Shalom

Shabbat shalom, Shabbat shalom,
Shabbat, Shabbat, Shabbat, Shabbat shalom!

Bim, bam, bim-bim-bim-bam, bim-bim-bim-bim-bam,
Shabbat shalom, Shabbat shalom,
Shabbat, Shabbat, Shabbat, Shabbat shalom!

Mah Yafeh HaYom

מַה יָפֶה הַיוֹם, שַׁבָּת שָׁלוֹם.

Mah yafeh hayom, Shabbat shalom.

How lovely today is, Shabbat shalom.

Shir Chadash

שִׁירוּ לַייָ כָּל־הָאָרֶץ,
שִׁירוּ לַייָ שִׁיר חָדָשׁ.

*Shiru l'Adonai kol haaretz,
shiru l'Adonai shir chadash.*

Sing unto God, all the earth, a new song.
I will sing unto God a new song.
Sing unto God and we'll all sing along,
all the earth, a new song, unto God.
(Julie Silver, based on Psalm 96:1)

Hineih Mah Tov

הִנֵּה מַה־טּוֹב וּמַה־נָּעִים
שֶׁבֶת אַחִים גַּם־יָחַד.

*Hineih mah tov u'mah na-im
shevet achim gam yachad.*

How good and how pleasant it is
that brothers and sisters dwell together.
(Psalm 133:1)

קַבָּלַת שַׁבָּת
KABBALAT SHABBAT
WELCOMING SHABBAT

עֶרֶב שַׁבָּת
EREV SHABBAT
FRIDAY
EVENING

Hadlakat Nerot הַדְלָקַת נֵרוֹת
Candle Blessing

בָּרוּךְ אַתָּה, יְיָ
אֱלֹהֵינוּ, מֶלֶךְ הָעוֹלָם,
אֲשֶׁר קִדְּשָׁנוּ בְּמִצְוֹתָיו,
וְצִוָּנוּ לְהַדְלִיק
נֵר שֶׁל שַׁבָּת.

*Baruch atah, Adonai
Eloheinu, Melech haolam,
asher kid'shanu b'mitzvotav,
v'tzivanu l'hadlik
ner shel Shabbat.*

Baruch atah, Adonai
our God, Ruler of the universe,
who makes us holy with mitzvot,
and who teaches us
to kindle the lights of Shabbat.

6

עֶרֶב שַׁבָּת
EREV SHABBAT
FRIDAY EVENING

Shabbat is . . .
flickering candles, sweet twisted challah, juice that makes my nose tickle,
giggling with my friends, a smile from the rabbi, sprinkled cookies at the Oneg.

Shabbat is . . .
sleeping in late, singing prayers to God, playing with tzitzit strings,
dancing behind the Torah, bagels with cream cheese.

Shabbat is . . .
lazy afternoons, ball games on the field,
snuggling with the people I love, remembering the miracles of creation.

L'chah Dodi לְכָה דוֹדִי
Welcoming the Shabbat Bride

עֶרֶב שַׁבָּת
EREV SHABBAT
FRIDAY
EVENING

לְכָה דוֹדִי לִקְרַאת כַּלָּה,
פְּנֵי שַׁבָּת נְקַבְּלָה.

*L'chah dodi likrat kalah,
p'nei Shabbat n'kab'lah.*

My love, come to meet the Shabbat bride;
my love, come to greet Shabbat.

(The Evening Service continues on page 18 with the Bar'chu.)

הדלקת נרות
Hadlakat Nerot

לְכָה דוֹדִי
L'chah Dodi

8

Mah Tovu מַה־טֹּבוּ
How Beautiful!

שַׁחֲרִית לְשַׁבָּת
SHACHARIT L'SHABBAT
SHABBAT MORNING

מַה־טֹּבוּ אֹהָלֶיךָ, יַעֲקֹב,
מִשְׁכְּנֹתֶיךָ, יִשְׂרָאֵל!

*Mah tovu ohalecha, Yaakov,
mishk'notecha Yisrael!*

How beautiful are your tents, O Jacob,
your dwelling places, O Israel!

מַה־טֹּבוּ
Mah Tovu

אֱלֹהַי נְשָׁמָה
Elohai N'shamah

אֲשֶׁר יָצַר
Asher Yatzar

נִסִּים בְּכָל יוֹם
Nisim B'chol Yom

מִזְמוֹר
Mizmor

שַׁחֲרִית לְשַׁבָּת
SHACHARIT L'SHABBAT
SHABBAT MORNING

Elohai N'shamah אֱלֹהַי נְשָׁמָה
The Soul That You Have Breathed Into Me

אֱלֹהַי, נְשָׁמָה שֶׁנָּתַתָּ בִּי טְהוֹרָה הִיא.

Elohai, n'shamah shenatata bi t'horah hi.

My God, the soul that You have breathed into me is pure.

בָּרוּךְ אַתָּה, יְיָ, אֲשֶׁר בְּיָדוֹ נֶפֶשׁ כָּל חַי וְרוּחַ כָּל בְּשַׂר אִישׁ.

Baruch atah, Adonai, asher b'yado nefesh kol chai v'ruach kol b'sar ish.

Baruch atah, Adonai, in whose hand is every living soul and the breath of all people.

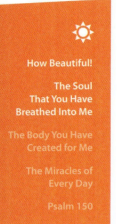

How Beautiful!
The Soul That You Have Breathed Into Me
The Body You Have Created for Me
The Miracles of Every Day
Psalm 150

11

Asher Yatzar אֲשֶׁר יָצַר
The Body You Have Created for Me

שַׁחֲרִית לְשַׁבָּת
SHACHARIT L'SHABBAT
SHABBAT MORNING

בָּרוּךְ אַתָּה, יְיָ אֱלֹהֵינוּ, מֶלֶךְ הָעוֹלָם,
אֲשֶׁר יָצַר אֶת הָאָדָם בְּחָכְמָה.

*Baruch atah, Adonai Eloheinu, Melech haolam,
asher yatzar et haadam b'chochmah.*

Praise to You, Adonai our God, Ruler of the universe,
who uses creativity and wisdom to make people.
Our hearts pump, our blood flows, and our minds think.
How amazing is this body You have created!

בָּרוּךְ אַתָּה, יְיָ, רוֹפֵא כָל בָּשָׂר וּמַפְלִיא לַעֲשׂוֹת.

Baruch atah, Adonai, rofei chol basar umafli laasot.

Baruch atah, Adonai, who helps us heal the sick
and creates bodies with wonder!

מַה־טֹּבוּ
Mah Tovu

אֱלֹהַי נְשָׁמָה
Elohai N'shamah

אֲשֶׁר יָצַר
Asher Yatzar

נִסִּים בְּכָל יוֹם
Nisim B'chol Yom

מִזְמוֹר
Mizmor

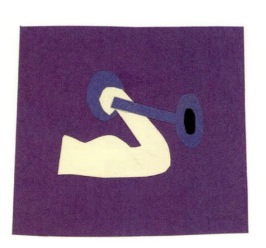

12

שַׁחֲרִית לְשַׁבָּת
SHACHARIT L'SHABBAT
SHABBAT MORNING

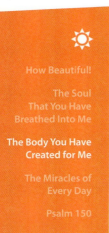

How Beautiful!

The Soul That You Have Breathed Into Me

The Body You Have Created for Me

The Miracles of Every Day

Psalm 150

I sometimes imagine God sitting
on the soft grass in the Garden of Eden
with art supplies scattered about.
Glue and paper,
Clay and crayons,
Colored yarn and colored sand.

God cuts and pastes
Imagines and draws
Pushes and forms the clay into the perfect shape.

I imagine that this is how God made people.
Carefully and creatively, paying attention to every detail,
God formed
Minds that think,
Hearts that pump,
Lungs that breathe,
and bodies that move.

How amazing is this body that You have created for me Adonai!

Baruch atah, Adonai, who helps us heal the sick and creates our bodies with wonder!

Nisim B'chol Yom נִסִּים בְּכָל יוֹם
The Miracles of Every Day

SHACHARIT L'SHABBAT
SHABBAT MORNING

בָּרוּךְ אַתָּה, יְיָ אֱלֹהֵינוּ, מֶלֶךְ הָעוֹלָם . . .

Baruch atah, Adonai Eloheinu, Melech haolam . . .

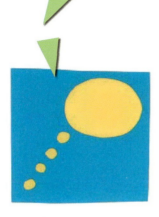
who gives us a mind.

who opens our eyes.

who makes people free.

Mah Tovu

Elohai N'shamah

Asher Yatzar

Nisim B'chol Yom

Mizmor

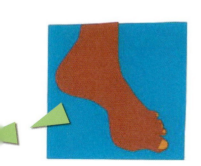
who strengthens our steps.

who stretches the earth over the waters.

who lifts us up.

שַׁחֲרִית לְשַׁבָּת
SHACHARIT L'SHABBAT
SHABBAT MORNING

How Beautiful!

The Soul That You Have Breathed Into Me

The Body You Have Created for Me

The Miracles of Every Day

Psalm 150

who makes Israel beautiful.   who makes Israel strong.   who makes us a Jewish family.

who makes us in God's image.   who makes me free.

who wakes us up.   who gives us strength.   who gives us clothes.

15

Mizmor מִזְמוֹר
Psalm 150

הַלְלוּ־יָהּ!

Hal'luyah!

Halleluyah!
Celebrate Life with blasts of the horn,
Celebrate Life with the strum of the harp,
Celebrate Life with tambourine and dance,
Celebrate Life with flute and cymbals.

כֹּל הַנְּשָׁמָה תְּהַלֵּל יָהּ,
הַלְלוּ־יָהּ!

Kol han'shamah t'haleil Yah,
Hal'luyah!

Let all that breathes praise God!
Halleluyah!

שַׁחֲרִית לְשַׁבָּת
SHACHARIT
L'SHABBAT
SHABBAT
MORNING

מַה־טֹּבוּ
Mah Tovu

אֱלֹהַי נְשָׁמָה
Elohai N'shamah

אֲשֶׁר יָצַר
Asher Yatzar

נִסִּים בְּכָל יוֹם
Nisim B'chol Yom

מִזְמוֹר
Mizmor

שַׁחֲרִית לְשַׁבָּת
SHACHARIT L'SHABBAT
SHABBAT MORNING

How Beautiful!

The Soul That You Have Breathed Into Me

The Body You Have Created for Me

The Miracles of Every Day

Psalm 150

כֹּל הַנְּשָׁמָה תְּהַלֵּל יָהּ, הַלְלוּ־יָהּ!

Kol han'shamah t'haleil Yah, Hal'luyah!

Let all that breathes praise God! Halleluyah!

Bar'chu בָּרְכוּ
Getting Ready to Pray

בָּרְכוּ אֶת יְיָ הַמְבֹרָךְ!
בָּרוּךְ יְיָ הַמְבֹרָךְ
לְעוֹלָם וָעֶד!

Bar'chu et Adonai ham'vorach!
Baruch Adonai ham'vorach
l'olam va-ed!

Praise Adonai to whom praise is due forever!
Praised be Adonai to whom praise is due,
now and forever!

שְׁמַע
וּבְרְכוֹתֶיהָ
SH'MA
UVIRCHOTEHA
THE SH'MA
AND ITS
BLESSINGS

בָּרְכוּ
Bar'chu

מַעֲרִיב עֲרָבִים
Maariv Aravim

יוֹצֵר אוֹר
Yotzeir Or

אַהֲבַת עוֹלָם
Ahavat Olam

אַהֲבָה רַבָּה
Ahavah Rabbah

שְׁמַע
Sh'ma

וְאָהַבְתָּ
V'ahavta

מִי כָמֹכָה
Mi Chamochah

הַשְׁכִּיבֵנוּ
Hashkiveinu

וְשָׁמְרוּ
V'shamru

שְׁמַע
וּבְרְכוֹתֶיהָ
***SH'MA
UVIRCHOTEHA***

THE SH'MA
AND ITS
BLESSINGS

**Getting Ready
to Pray**

Who Creates
the Night

Who Creates Light

With Great Love

God's Love

Sh'ma

You Shall Love

Who Is Like You?

Tuck Us In

Keep Shabbat

How do you get ready to pray?
Do you close your eyes,
or do you look around the room at everyone who
 loves you?

Do you breathe out and let your body relax,
or do you breathe in the sweet smells of challah
 and wine?

Do you look to the sky and search for God,
or do you look at the earth to see beauty in the
 world around you?

How do you get ready to pray?

Maariv Aravim מַעֲרִיב עֲרָבִים
Who Creates the Night

בָּרוּךְ אַתָּה, יְיָ
אֱלֹהֵינוּ, מֶלֶךְ הָעוֹלָם,
אֲשֶׁר בִּדְבָרוֹ מַעֲרִיב עֲרָבִים.

*Baruch atah, Adonai
Eloheinu, Melech haolam,
asher bid'varo maariv aravim.*

Blessed are You, Adonai our God,
Ruler of the universe, who spoke and created the night.
You put the stars in the sky and created day and night.
You roll the light away from the darkness,
and the darkness away from the light.

בָּרוּךְ אַתָּה, יְיָ, הַמַּעֲרִיב עֲרָבִים.

Baruch atah, Adonai, hamaariv aravim.

Baruch atah, Adonai, who creates the night.

(The Evening Service continues on page 24 with Ahavat Olam.)

שְׁמַע
וּבִרְכוֹתֶיהָ
SH'MA
UVIRCHOTEHA
THE SH'MA
AND ITS
BLESSINGS

בָּרְכוּ
Bar'chu

מַעֲרִיב עֲרָבִים
Maariv Aravim

יוֹצֵר אוֹר
Yotzeir Or

אַהֲבַת עוֹלָם
Ahavat Olam

אַהֲבָה רַבָּה
Ahavah Rabbah

שְׁמַע
Sh'ma

וְאָהַבְתָּ
V'ahavta

מִי כָמֹכָה
Mi Chamochah

הַשְׁכִּיבֵנוּ
Hashkiveinu

וְשָׁמְרוּ
V'shamru

שְׁמַע
וּבִרְכוֹתֶיהָ
SH'MA UVIRCHOTEHA
THE SH'MA AND ITS BLESSINGS

Getting Ready to Pray
Who Creates the Night
Who Creates Light
With Great Love
God's Love
Sh'ma
You Shall Love
Who Is Like You?
Tuck Us In
Keep Shabbat

Who paints the world?
Who finds the perfect colors?

The orange of the sun.
The white of the clouds.
The red of the bird's feathers.

Who paints the world?
Who finds the perfect colors?

The silver of the stars.
The gray of the moon.
The yellow of the owl's eyes.

God is the Artist who loves to paint the world.
God is the One who finds the perfect colors.

God is the One who mixes the blue of the day
with the black of the night
and creates the beautiful colors of the evening.

בָּרוּךְ אַתָּה, יְיָ, הַמַּעֲרִיב עֲרָבִים.

Baruch atah, Adonai, hamaariv aravim.

Baruch atah, Adonai, who creates the night.

Yotzeir Or יוֹצֵר אוֹר
Who Creates Light

בָּרוּךְ אַתָּה, יְיָ אֱלֹהֵינוּ, מֶלֶךְ הָעוֹלָם,
יוֹצֵר אוֹר וּבוֹרֵא חֹשֶׁךְ,
עֹשֶׂה שָׁלוֹם וּבוֹרֵא אֶת־הַכֹּל.

*Baruch atah, Adonai Eloheinu, Melech haolam,
yotzeir or uvorei choshech,
oseh shalom uvorei et ha-kol.*

Blessed are You, Adonai our God, Ruler of the universe, Creator of light and darkness, who makes peace and creates all things.

בָּרוּךְ אַתָּה, יְיָ, יוֹצֵר הַמְּאוֹרוֹת.

Baruch atah, Adonai, yotzeir ham'orot.

Baruch atah, Adonai, Creator of the lights in the sky.

(The Morning Service continues on page 26 with Ahavah Rabbah.)

שְׁמַע
וּבְרְכוֹתֶיהָ
SH'MA UVIRCHOTEHA

THE SH'MA AND ITS BLESSINGS

Getting Ready to Pray
Who Creates the Night
Who Creates Light
With Great Love
God's Love
Sh'ma
You Shall Love
Who Is Like You?
Tuck Us In
Keep Shabbat

The sun rises and the black of the night fades away.
Brilliant oranges, pinks, and yellows fill the sky.
Blessed is the Light of Day.

Animals slowly wake, squinting in the sun,
running, squirming, and sniffing through the grass.
Blessed is the Light of Creation.

People reach out to each other,
helping, supporting, and loving one another.
Blessed is the Light of Peace.

Baruch atah, Adonai:
Blessed is the Light of the World.

בָּרוּךְ אַתָּה, יְיָ, יוֹצֵר הַמְּאוֹרוֹת.

Baruch atah, Adonai, yotzeir ham'orot.

Baruch atah, Adonai, Creator of the lights in the sky.

Ahavat Olam אַהֲבַת עוֹלָם
With Great Love

אַהֲבַת עוֹלָם
בֵּית יִשְׂרָאֵל עַמְּךָ אָהָבְתָּ,
תּוֹרָה וּמִצְוֹת,
חֻקִּים וּמִשְׁפָּטִים, אוֹתָנוּ לִמַּדְתָּ.

Ahavat olam
beit Yisrael amcha ahavta,
Torah umitzvot,
chukim umishpatim, otanu limadta.

With great love, God,
You love Your people Israel.
You teach us Torah and mitzvot
and give us laws and rules to live by.

בָּרוּךְ אַתָּה, יְיָ, אוֹהֵב עַמּוֹ יִשְׂרָאֵל.

Baruch atah, Adonai, ohev amo Yisrael.

Baruch atah, Adonai, who loves Your people Israel.

שְׁמַע
וּבִרְכוֹתֶיהָ
SH'MA
UVIRCHOTEHA
THE SH'MA
AND ITS
BLESSINGS

בָּרְכוּ
Bar'chu

מַעֲרִיב עֲרָבִים
Maariv Aravim

יוֹצֵר אוֹר
Yotzeir Or

אַהֲבַת עוֹלָם
Ahavat Olam

אַהֲבָה רַבָּה
Ahavah Rabbah

שְׁמַע
Sh'ma

וְאָהַבְתָּ
V'ahavta

מִי כָמֹכָה
Mi Chamochah

הַשְׁכִּיבֵנוּ
Hashkiveinu

וְשָׁמְרוּ
V'shamru

שְׁמַע
וּבְרְכוֹתֶיהָ
SH'MA
UVIRCHOTEHA
THE SH'MA
AND ITS
BLESSINGS

Getting Ready to Pray
Who Creates the Night
Who Creates Light
With Great Love
God's Love
Sh'ma
You Shall Love
Who Is Like You?
Tuck Us In
Keep Shabbat

God is the hug you get from a friend and the kiss on your head from a parent.
God is the "good job" from a coach.

God is Love in the world.

God is the color of fall leaves and the cool water when you dip your hands in a river.
God is the sweet smell of spring flowers.

God is Love in the world.

God is the good-night kiss you give to someone you love and the smile for a new friend.
God is the "thank you" you give to a teacher of Torah.

God is Love in the world.

בָּרוּךְ אַתָּה, יְיָ, אוֹהֵב עַמּוֹ יִשְׂרָאֵל.

Baruch atah, Adonai, ohev amo Yisrael.

Baruch atah, Adonai, who loves Your people Israel.

Ahavah Rabbah אַהֲבָה רַבָּה
God's Love

אַהֲבָה רַבָּה אֲהַבְתָּנוּ, יְיָ אֱלֹהֵינוּ,
חֶמְלָה גְדוֹלָה וִיתֵרָה חָמַלְתָּ עָלֵינוּ.

*Ahavah rabbah ahavtanu, Adonai Eloheinu,
chemlah g'dolah viteirah chamalta aleinu.*

You love us, Adonai our God, like You loved our ancestors. They trusted You, and You taught them Your Torah. Teach us Your Torah, too, and make Your laws a part of our life.

בָּרוּךְ אַתָּה, יְיָ, הַבּוֹחֵר בְּעַמּוֹ יִשְׂרָאֵל בְּאַהֲבָה.

Baruch atah, Adonai, habocheir b'amo Yisrael b'ahavah.

Baruch atah, Adonai,
who chooses Your people Israel with love.

שְׁמַע
וּבְרְכוֹתֶיהָ
**SH'MA
UVIRCHOTEHA**

**THE SH'MA
AND ITS
BLESSINGS**

Getting Ready
to Pray

Who Creates
the Night

Who Creates Light

With Great Love

God's Love

Sh'ma

You Shall Love

Who Is Like You?

Tuck Us In

Keep Shabbat

בָּרוּךְ אַתָּה, יְיָ, הַבּוֹחֵר בְּעַמּוֹ יִשְׂרָאֵל בְּאַהֲבָה.

Baruch atah, Adonai, habocheir b'amo Yisrael b'ahavah.

Baruch atah, Adonai,
who chooses Your people Israel with love.

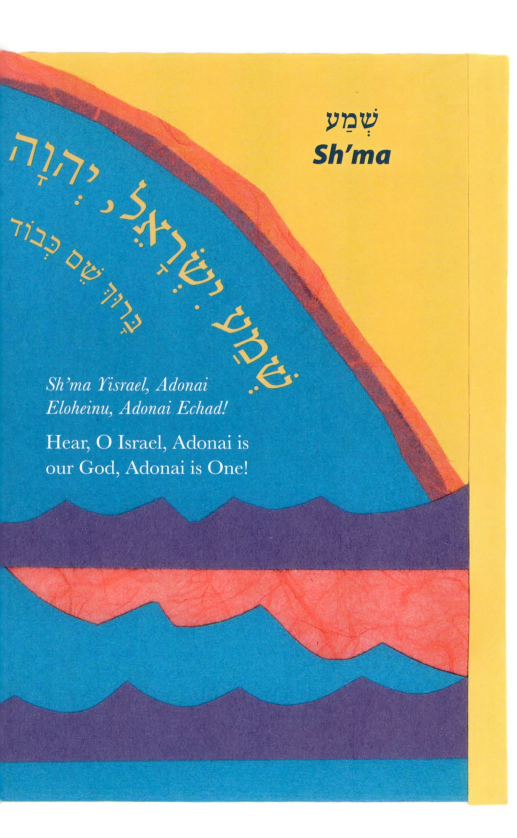

שְׁמַע
Sh'ma

Sh'ma Yisrael, Adonai Eloheinu, Adonai Echad!

Hear, O Israel, Adonai is our God, Adonai is One!

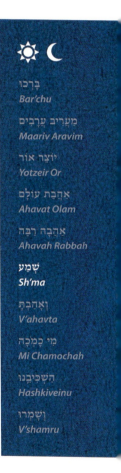

שְׁמַע וּבִרְכוֹתֶיהָ
SH'MA UVIRCHOTEHA
THE SH'MA AND ITS BLESSINGS

בָּרְכוּ
Bar'chu

מַעֲרִיב עֲרָבִים
Maariv Aravim

יוֹצֵר אוֹר
Yotzeir Or

אַהֲבַת עוֹלָם
Ahavat Olam

אַהֲבָה רַבָּה
Ahavah Rabbah

שְׁמַע
Sh'ma

וְאָהַבְתָּ
V'ahavta

מִי כָמֹכָה
Mi Chamochah

הַשְׁכִּיבֵנוּ
Hashkiveinu

וְשָׁמְרוּ
V'shamru

שְׁמַע וּבְרְכוֹתֶיהָ
SH'MA UVIRCHOTEHA

THE SH'MA AND ITS BLESSINGS

Getting Ready to Pray
Who Creates the Night
Who Creates Light
With Great Love
God's Love
Sh'ma
You Shall Love
Who Is Like You?
Tuck Us In
Keep Shabbat

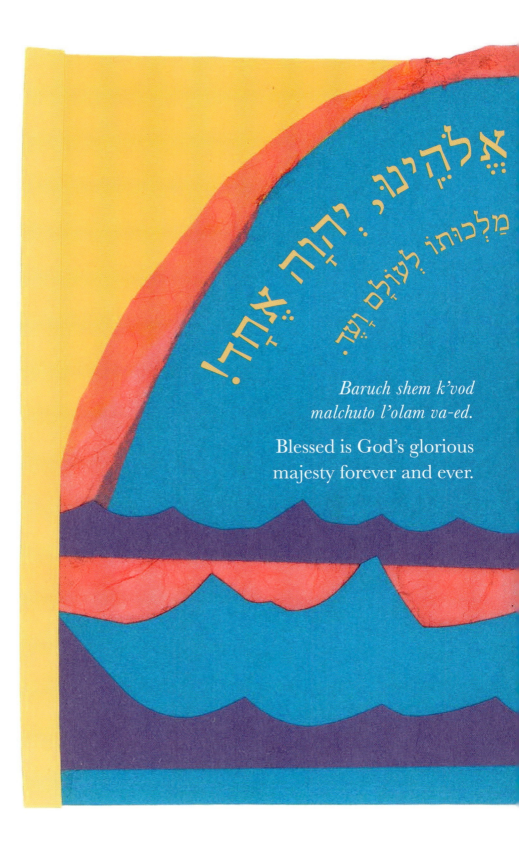

אֱלֹהֵינוּ, יְהֹוָה מַלְכוּתוֹ לְעוֹלָם וָעֶד אֶחָד!

Baruch shem k'vod malchuto l'olam va-ed.

Blessed is God's glorious majesty forever and ever.

V'ahavta וְאָהַבְתָּ
You Shall Love

וְאָהַבְתָּ אֵת יְיָ אֱלֹהֶיךָ,
בְּכָל־לְבָבְךָ, וּבְכָל־נַפְשְׁךָ, וּבְכָל־מְאֹדֶךָ.

*V'ahavta eit Adonai Elohecha, b'chol l'vav'cha,
uv'chol nafsh'cha, uv'chol m'odecha.*

Love Adonai your God, with all your heart,
with all your soul, with all your might.
Take these words that I command today
and keep them in your heart.
Teach them to your children.
Talk about them in your home and on your way,
before you go to sleep and when you wake up.
Put them as a special sign on your hand,
and make them a symbol on your forehead.
Write them on the doorposts of your house
and on your gates.

Remember and follow all of My commandments,
and be a holy people for your God.
I am Adonai, who freed you from slavery in Egypt
to be your God.

יְיָ אֱלֹהֵיכֶם אֱמֶת.

Adonai Eloheichem emet.

I am Adonai your God.

שְׁמַע
וּבְרְכוֹתֶיהָ
SH'MA
UVIRCHOTEHA
THE SH'MA
AND ITS
BLESSINGS

בָּרְכוּ
Bar'chu

מַעֲרִיב עֲרָבִים
Maariv Aravim

יוֹצֵר אוֹר
Yotzeir Or

אַהֲבַת עוֹלָם
Ahavat Olam

אַהֲבָה רַבָּה
Ahavah Rabbah

שְׁמַע
Sh'ma

וְאָהַבְתָּ
V'ahavta

מִי כָמֹכָה
Mi Chamochah

הַשְׁכִּיבֵנוּ
Hashkiveinu

וְשָׁמְרוּ
V'shamru

שְׁמַע
וּבִרְכוֹתֶיהָ
**SH'MA
UVIRCHOTEHA**
THE SH'MA
AND ITS
BLESSINGS

Getting Ready to Pray
Who Creates the Night
Who Creates Light
With Great Love
God's Love
Sh'ma
You Shall Love
Who Is Like You?
Tuck Us In
Keep Shabbat

יְיָ אֱלֹהֵיכֶם אֱמֶת.

Adonai Eloheichem emet.

I am Adonai your God.

31

Mi Chamochah מִי כָמֹכָה
Who Is Like You?

מִי־כָמֹכָה בָּאֵלִם, יְיָ!
מִי כָּמֹכָה נֶאְדָּר בַּקֹּדֶשׁ, נוֹרָא תְהִלֹּת, עֹשֵׂה פֶלֶא!

Mi chamochah ba-eilim, Adonai!
Mi kamochah nedar bakodesh, nora t'hilot, oseih fele!

Who is like You, Adonai?
Who is like You, holy and awesome, working wonders?

בָּרוּךְ אַתָּה, יְיָ, גָּאַל יִשְׂרָאֵל.

Baruch atah, Adonai, gaal Yisrael.

Baruch atah, Adonai, who rescues the people Israel.

שְׁמַע וּבִרְכוֹתֶיהָ
SH'MA UVIRCHOTEHA
THE SH'MA AND ITS BLESSINGS

בָּרְכוּ
Bar'chu

מַעֲרִיב עֲרָבִים
Maariv Aravim

יוֹצֵר אוֹר
Yotzeir Or

אַהֲבַת עוֹלָם
Ahavat Olam

אַהֲבָה רַבָּה
Ahavah Rabbah

שְׁמַע
Sh'ma

וְאָהַבְתָּ
V'ahavta

מִי כָמֹכָה
Mi Chamochah

הַשְׁכִּיבֵנוּ
Hashkiveinu

וְשָׁמְרוּ
V'shamru

שְׁמַע
וּבְרְכוֹתֶיהָ

SH'MA UVIRCHOTEHA

THE SH'MA AND ITS BLESSINGS

We remember when we were slaves in Egypt.
We remember when the Egyptians forced us to work from sunrise to sunset.
We remember when our bellies growled because there was no food to eat.
We remember when all we wanted was a cool drink of water.
We remember when we had no warm blankets and shivered in the night.

We remember crossing into safety and breathing the air of freedom.
We remember dancing with joy and singing our song of thanks.

And because we remember, we promise this day
 to feed the hungry
 to bring water to the thirsty
 to give clothes to the needy
 and to reach out our hands and bring the whole world into our freedom dance.

בָּרוּךְ אַתָּה, יְיָ, גָּאַל יִשְׂרָאֵל.

Baruch atah, Adonai, gaal Yisrael.

Baruch atah, Adonai, who rescues the people Israel.

(The Morning Service continues on page 38 with the T'filah.)

Hashkiveinu הַשְׁכִּיבֵנוּ
Tuck Us In

הַשְׁכִּיבֵנוּ, יְיָ אֱלֹהֵינוּ,
לְשָׁלוֹם, וְהַעֲמִידֵנוּ שׁוֹמְרֵנוּ לְחַיִּים.

*Hashkiveinu, Adonai Eloheinu,
l'shalom, v'haamideinu shom'reinu l'chayim.*

Tuck us into our beds, Adonai our God,
and wake us up feeling strong and healthy.

וּפְרֹשׂ עָלֵינוּ סֻכַּת שְׁלוֹמֶךָ.

Ufros aleinu sukat sh'lomecha.

Spread over us Your blanket of peace.

בָּרוּךְ אַתָּה, יְיָ, הַפּוֹרֵשׂ סֻכַּת שָׁלוֹם עָלֵינוּ וְעַל כָּל
עַמּוֹ יִשְׂרָאֵל וְעַל יְרוּשָׁלָיִם.

*Baruch atah, Adonai, haporeis sukat shalom aleinu v'al kol
amo Yisrael v'al Y'rushalayim.*

Baruch atah, Adonai,
who spreads Your blanket of peace over us,
over all Your people, and over Jerusalem.

בָּרוּךְ אַתָּה, יְיָ, הַפּוֹרֵשׂ סֻכַּת שָׁלוֹם עָלֵינוּ וְעַל כָּל עַמּוֹ יִשְׂרָאֵל וְעַל יְרוּשָׁלָיִם.

Baruch atah, Adonai, haporeis sukat shalom aleinu v'al kol amo Yisrael v'al Y'rushalayim.

Baruch atah, Adonai, who spreads Your blanket of peace over us, over all Your people, and over Jerusalem.

V'shamru וְשָׁמְרוּ
Keep Shabbat

וְשָׁמְרוּ בְנֵי יִשְׂרָאֵל אֶת־הַשַּׁבָּת,
לַעֲשׂוֹת אֶת־הַשַּׁבָּת לְדֹרֹתָם בְּרִית עוֹלָם.

*V'shamru v'nei Yisrael et HaShabbat,
laasot et HaShabbat l'dorotam b'rit olam.*

The people of Israel shall keep Shabbat,
celebrating Shabbat for all time.

שְׁמַע
וּבִרְכוֹתֶיהָ
SH'MA
UVIRCHOTEHA
THE SH'MA
AND ITS
BLESSINGS

בָּרְכוּ
Bar'chu

מַעֲרִיב עֲרָבִים
Maariv Aravim

יוֹצֵר אוֹר
Yotzeir Or

אַהֲבַת עוֹלָם
Ahavat Olam

אַהֲבָה רַבָּה
Ahavah Rabbah

שְׁמַע
Sh'ma

וְאָהַבְתָּ
V'ahavta

מִי כָמֹכָה
Mi Chamochah

הַשְׁכִּיבֵנוּ
Hashkiveinu

וְשָׁמְרוּ
V'shamru

שְׁמַע
וּבְרְכוֹתֶיהָ
SH'MA
UVIRCHOTEHA
THE SH'MA
AND ITS
BLESSINGS

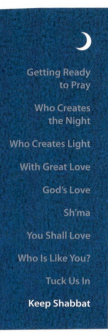

Getting Ready to Pray
Who Creates the Night
Who Creates Light
With Great Love
God's Love
Sh'ma
You Shall Love
Who Is Like You?
Tuck Us In
Keep Shabbat

V'shamru v'nei Yisrael—the people of Israel shall celebrate Shabbat in every generation.

We gather with grandmas and grandpas.
Snuggled close,
we light Shabbat candles.

We stand beside mothers and fathers, aunts and uncles.
With their hands upon our heads,
we light Shabbat candles.

Shoulder to shoulder with brothers and sisters,
sharing smiles and giggles
we light Shabbat candles.

And someday when we are grown up,
we will stand with our children
and will light Shabbat candles.

V'shamru v'nei Yisrael—the people of Israel shall celebrate Shabbat in every generation.

Kavanah כַּוָּנָה
Time to Prepare

תְּפִלָּה
T'FILAH
OUR PRAYER

אֲדֹנָי, שְׂפָתַי תִּפְתָּח,
וּפִי יַגִּיד תְּהִלָּתֶךָ.

*Adonai s'fatai tiftach,
ufi yagid t'hilatecha.*

Adonai, open my mouth
so that I can pray to You with all my heart.

כַּוָּנָה
Kavanah

אָבוֹת וְאִמָּהוֹת
Avot V'Imahot

גְּבוּרוֹת
G'vurot

קְדֻשָּׁה
K'dushah

קְדֻשַּׁת הַיּוֹם
K'dushat HaYom

עֲבוֹדָה
Avodah

הוֹדָאָה
Hodaah

שָׁלוֹם
Shalom

תְּפִלַת הַלֵּב
T'filat HaLev

38

תְּפִלָּה
T'FILAH
OUR PRAYER

Time to Prepare
Our Fathers and Our Mothers
God's Power
You Are Holy
This Holy Day
The Work of Prayer
Praise
Peace
Prayers of the Heart

Adonai, our God, You are the Protector of Abraham and the One who remembers Sarah.

You watched over their children and their children's children.

You were their strength, and with Your help they were able to do great things. They called You the Holy God and knew that You were with them whenever they needed You.

Help me, God, to also know You.

Help me to be strong and brave.

Teach me to be holy.

Let me rest each Shabbat, and help me see the beautiful world around me.

Help me find the words to thank You, Adonai my God.

Teach me Your peace, and help me be a peacemaker for all the world.

Avot V'Imahot אָבוֹת וְאִמָּהוֹת
Our Fathers and Our Mothers

בָּרוּךְ אַתָּה, יְיָ אֱלֹהֵינוּ
וֵאלֹהֵי אֲבוֹתֵינוּ וְאִמּוֹתֵינוּ,
אֱלֹהֵי אַבְרָהָם, אֱלֹהֵי יִצְחָק, וֵאלֹהֵי יַעֲקֹב,
אֱלֹהֵי שָׂרָה, אֱלֹהֵי רִבְקָה,
אֱלֹהֵי רָחֵל וֵאלֹהֵי לֵאָה.

*Baruch atah, Adonai Eloheinu
veilohei avoteinu v'imoteinu,
Elohei Avraham, Elohei Yitzchak veilohei Yaakov,
Elohei Sarah, Elohei Rivkah,
Elohei Rachel veilohei Leah.*

Blessed are You, Adonai our God
and the God of our fathers and mothers.
You are the God of Abraham,
the God of Isaac, the God of Jacob,
the God of Sarah, the God of Rebecca,
the God of Rachel, and the God of Leah.

בָּרוּךְ אַתָּה, יְיָ, מָגֵן אַבְרָהָם וְעֶזְרַת שָׂרָה.

Baruch atah, Adonai, magein Avraham v'ezrat Sarah.

Baruch atah, Adonai,
Abraham's Shield and Sarah's Helper.

תְּפִלָּה
T'FILAH
OUR PRAYER

כַּוָּנָה
Kavanah

אָבוֹת וְאִמָּהוֹת
Avot V'Imahot

גְּבוּרוֹת
G'vurot

קְדֻשָּׁה
K'dushah

קְדֻשַּׁת הַיּוֹם
K'dushat HaYom

עֲבוֹדָה
Avodah

הוֹדָאָה
Hodaah

שָׁלוֹם
Shalom

תְּפִלַּת הַלֵּב
T'filat HaLev

40

תְּפִלָּה
T'FILAH
OUR PRAYER

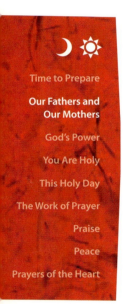

Time to Prepare

Our Fathers and Our Mothers

God's Power

You Are Holy

This Holy Day

The Work of Prayer

Praise

Peace

Prayers of the Heart

בָּרוּךְ אַתָּה, יְיָ, מָגֵן אַבְרָהָם וְעֶזְרַת שָׂרָה.

Baruch atah, Adonai, magein Avraham v'ezrat Sarah.

Baruch atah, Adonai,
Abraham's Shield and Sarah's Helper.

G'vurot גְּבוּרוֹת
God's Power

אַתָּה גִּבּוֹר לְעוֹלָם, אֲדֹנָי,
מְחַיֵּה הַכֹּל [מֵתִים] אַתָּה,
רַב לְהוֹשִׁיעַ.

Atah gibor l'olam, Adonai,
m'chayeih hakol [meitim] atah,
rav l'hoshia.

You are forever mighty, Adonai. You give life to all.
[Winter] You cause the winds to blow and the rain to fall.
[Summer] Your dew helps the earth to grow.
Who is like You, Source of Power in the world?

בָּרוּךְ אַתָּה, יְיָ, מְחַיֵּה הַכֹּל [הַמֵּתִים].

Baruch atah, Adonai, m'chayeih hakol [hameitim].

Baruch atah, Adonai, who gives life to all.

תְּפִלָּה
T'FILAH
OUR PRAYER

Kavanah
Avot V'Imahot
G'vurot
K'dushah
K'dushat HaYom
Avodah
Hodaah
Shalom
T'filat HaLev

42

בָּרוּךְ אַתָּה, יְיָ, מְחַיֵּה הַכֹּל [הַמֵּתִים].

Baruch atah, Adonai, m'chayeih hakol [hameitim].

Baruch atah, Adonai, who gives life to all.

Evening K'dushah קְדֻשָּׁה
You Are Holy

אַתָּה קָדוֹשׁ וְשִׁמְךָ קָדוֹשׁ
וּקְדוֹשִׁים בְּכָל יוֹם יְהַלְלוּךָ, סֶלָה.

*Atah kadosh v'shimcha kadosh
uk'doshim b'chol yom y'hal'lucha, selah.*

You are holy, God. Your Name is holy.
Those who are holy praise Your Name every day.

בָּרוּךְ אַתָּה, יְיָ, הָאֵל הַקָּדוֹשׁ.

Baruch atah, Adonai, Ha-El HaKadosh.

Baruch atah, Adonai, the Holy God.

תְּפִלָּה
T'FILAH
OUR PRAYER

כַּוָּנָה
Kavanah

אָבוֹת וְאִמָּהוֹת
Avot V'Imahot

גְּבוּרוֹת
G'vurot

קְדֻשָּׁה
K'dushah

קְדֻשַּׁת הַיּוֹם
K'dushat HaYom

עֲבוֹדָה
Avodah

הוֹדָאָה
Hodaah

שָׁלוֹם
Shalom

תְּפִלַּת הַלֵּב
T'filat HaLev

T'FILAH
OUR PRAYER
תְּפִלָּה

Morning K'dushah קְדֻשָּׁה
You Are Holy

קָדוֹשׁ, קָדוֹשׁ, קָדוֹשׁ יְיָ צְבָאוֹת,
מְלֹא כָל הָאָרֶץ כְּבוֹדוֹ.

*Kadosh, kadosh, kadosh Adonai Tz'vaot,
m'lo chol haaretz k'vodo.*

Holy, holy, holy is Adonai Tz'vaot!
God's presence fills the whole earth!

Time to Prepare
Our Fathers and Our Mothers
God's Power
You Are Holy
This Holy Day
The Work of Prayer
Praise
Peace
Prayers of the Heart

Inside me is a holy spark:
a light that shines brightly when I feel proud of myself;
when I feel strong inside;
when I see the beautiful world around me.

Inside each of us is a holy spark:
lights that shine bright when we help one another;
when we are kind to people we don't even know;
when we take care of the world together.

Baruch atah, Adonai, the Holy Spark within us.

בָּרוּךְ אַתָּה, יְיָ, הָאֵל הַקָּדוֹשׁ.

Baruch atah, Adonai, Ha-El HaKadosh.

Baruch atah, Adonai, the Holy God.

K'dushat HaYom קְדֻשַּׁת הַיּוֹם
This Holy Day

בָּרוּךְ אַתָּה, יְיָ, מְקַדֵּשׁ הַשַּׁבָּת.

Baruch atah, Adonai, m'kadeish HaShabbat.

Baruch atah, Adonai, who makes Shabbat holy.

תְּפִלָּה
T'FILAH
OUR PRAYER

כַּוָּנָה
Kavanah

אָבוֹת וְאִמָּהוֹת
Avot V'Imahot

גְּבוּרוֹת
G'vurot

קְדֻשָּׁה
K'dushah

קְדֻשַּׁת הַיּוֹם
K'dushat HaYom

עֲבוֹדָה
Avodah

הוֹדָאָה
Hodaah

שָׁלוֹם
Shalom

תְּפִלַּת הַלֵּב
T'filat HaLev

תְּפִלָּה
T'FILAH
OUR PRAYER

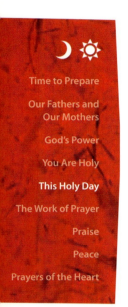

Time to Prepare
Our Fathers and Our Mothers
God's Power
You Are Holy
This Holy Day
The Work of Prayer
Praise
Peace
Prayers of the Heart

Today we thank You, God, for sabbath rest.

We thank You for lazy mornings and good books.

We thank You for laughter and time to play.

We thank You for dinners with our families and cookies with our friends.

We thank You for Sabbath song and celebration.

Blessed are you, Adonai, who makes the Sabbath holy.

Avodah עֲבוֹדָה
The Work of Prayer

רְצֵה, יְיָ אֱלֹהֵינוּ, בְּעַמְּךָ יִשְׂרָאֵל,
וּתְפִלָּתָם בְּאַהֲבָה תְקַבֵּל.

*R'tzei, Adonai Eloheinu, b'amcha Yisrael,
ut'filatam b'ahavah t'kabeil.*

Be happy, Adonai our God, with Your people Israel,
and accept our prayers with love.

תְּפִלָּה
T'FILAH
OUR PRAYER

כַּוָּנָה
Kavanah

אָבוֹת וְאִמָּהוֹת
Avot V'Imahot

גְּבוּרוֹת
G'vurot

קְדֻשָּׁה
K'dushah

קְדֻשַּׁת הַיּוֹם
K'dushat HaYom

עֲבוֹדָה
Avodah

הוֹדָאָה
Hodaah

שָׁלוֹם
Shalom

תְּפִלַּת הַלֵּב
T'filat HaLev

48

תְּפִלָּה
T'FILAH
OUR PRAYER

Hodaah הוֹדָאָה
Praise

מוֹדִים אֲנַחְנוּ לָךְ.

Modim anachnu lach.

We give thanks to You.

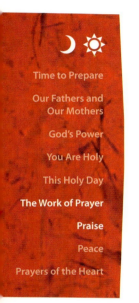

- Time to Prepare
- Our Fathers and Our Mothers
- God's Power
- You Are Holy
- This Holy Day
- The Work of Prayer
- **Praise**
- Peace
- Prayers of the Heart

Shalom שָׁלוֹם
Evening Prayer for Peace

תְּפִלָּה
T'FILAH
OUR PRAYER

שָׁלוֹם רָב עַל יִשְׂרָאֵל עַמְּךָ תָּשִׂים לְעוֹלָם.

Shalom rav al Yisrael amcha tasim l'olam.

Grant peace for Your people Israel and for all the world.

כַּוָּנָה
Kavanah

אָבוֹת וְאִמָּהוֹת
Avot V'Imahot

גְּבוּרוֹת
G'vurot

קְדֻשָּׁה
K'dushah

קְדֻשַּׁת הַיּוֹם
K'dushat HaYom

עֲבוֹדָה
Avodah

הוֹדָאָה
Hodaah

שָׁלוֹם
Shalom

תְּפִלַּת הַלֵּב
T'filat HaLev

תְּפִלָּה
T'FILAH
OUR PRAYER

Shalom שָׁלוֹם
Morning Prayer for Peace

שִׂים שָׁלוֹם טוֹבָה וּבְרָכָה, חֵן וָחֶסֶד
וְרַחֲמִים, עָלֵינוּ וְעַל כָּל יִשְׂרָאֵל עַמֶּךָ.

Sim shalom tovah uv'rachah, chein vachesed v'rachamim, aleinu v'al kol Yisrael amecha.

Grant peace, goodness, blessing, grace, kindness, and mercy on us and all of Your people, Israel.

Time to Prepare
Our Fathers and Our Mothers
God's Power
You Are Holy
This Holy Day
The Work of Prayer
Praise
Peace
Prayers of the Heart

T'filat HaLev תְּפִלַּת הַלֵּב
Prayers of the Heart

יִהְיוּ לְרָצוֹן אִמְרֵי פִי וְהֶגְיוֹן לִבִּי לְפָנֶיךָ,
יְיָ צוּרִי וְגוֹאֲלִי.

*Yih'yu l'ratzon imrei fi v'hegyon libi l'fanecha,
Adonai tzuri v'go-ali.*

May the words of my mouth
and what I think in my heart be good and kind.
God, You are always there to hear and help me.

עֹשֶׂה שָׁלוֹם בִּמְרוֹמָיו,
הוּא יַעֲשֶׂה שָׁלוֹם עָלֵינוּ,
וְעַל כָּל יִשְׂרָאֵל, וְאִמְרוּ: אָמֵן.

*Oseh shalom bimromav,
hu yaaseh shalom aleinu,
v'al kol Yisrael, v'imru: Amen.*

May the One who makes peace in the high heavens
make peace for us and for all of Israel, Amen.

(Reading of the Torah can be found on page 56.)
(The Concluding Prayers can be found on page 106.)

סֵדֶר קְרִיאַת הַתּוֹרָה
Reading of the Torah

In this scroll is the secret of our people's
life from Sinai until now.
Its teaching is love and justice,
goodness and hope.
Freedom is its gift to all who treasure it.

Kabbalat HaTorah קַבָּלַת הַתּוֹרָה
Receiving the Torah

שְׁמַע יִשְׂרָאֵל, יְיָ אֱלֹהֵינוּ, יְיָ אֶחָד.

Sh'ma Yisrael, Adonai Eloheinu, Adonai Echad.

Hear, O Israel, Adonai is our God, Adonai is One.

גַּדְּלוּ לַייָ אִתִּי,
וּנְרוֹמְמָה שְׁמוֹ יַחְדָּו.

*Gadlu l'Adonai iti,
un'rom'mah sh'mo yachdav.*

Praise God with me, let us praise God together.

קַבָּלַת הַתּוֹרָה
Kabbalat HaTorah

בִּרְכוֹת הַתּוֹרָה
Birchot HaTorah

סֵדֶר קְרִיאַת הַתּוֹרָה
SEDER K'RIAT HATORAH
READING THE TORAH

Birchot HaTorah בִּרְכוֹת הַתּוֹרָה
Blessings for Torah Readings

Blessing before the Reading of the Torah

בָּרְכוּ אֶת יְיָ הַמְבֹרָךְ.

Bar'chu et Adonai ham'vorach.

Praise Adonai, the blessed One.

בָּרוּךְ יְיָ הַמְבֹרָךְ לְעוֹלָם וָעֶד.

Baruch Adonai ham'vorach l'olam va-ed.

Praised is Adonai, the blessed One, now and forever.

בָּרוּךְ אַתָּה, יְיָ אֱלֹהֵינוּ, מֶלֶךְ הָעוֹלָם,
אֲשֶׁר בָּחַר בָּנוּ מִכָּל הָעַמִּים, וְנָתַן לָנוּ אֶת תּוֹרָתוֹ.
בָּרוּךְ אַתָּה, יְיָ, נוֹתֵן הַתּוֹרָה.

*Baruch atah, Adonai Eloheinu, Melech haolam,
asher bachar banu mikol haamim, v'natan lanu et Torato.
Baruch atah, Adonai, notein haTorah.*

Blessed are You, Adonai our God,
Ruler of the universe, who has chosen us
from among the peoples and given us the Torah.
Blessed are You, Adonai, who gives the Torah.

סֵדֶר קְרִיאַת הַתּוֹרָה
SEDER K'RIAT HATORAH
READING THE TORAH

קַבָּלַת הַתּוֹרָה
Kabbalat HaTorah

בִּרְכוֹת הַתּוֹרָה
Birchot HaTorah

סֵדֶר קְרִיאַת הַתּוֹרָה

SEDER K'RIAT HATORAH

READING THE TORAH

Receiving the Torah

Blessings for Torah Readings

Blessing after the Reading of the Torah

בָּרוּךְ אַתָּה, יְיָ אֱלֹהֵינוּ, מֶלֶךְ הָעוֹלָם,
אֲשֶׁר נָתַן לָנוּ תּוֹרַת אֱמֶת, וְחַיֵּי עוֹלָם נָטַע בְּתוֹכֵנוּ.
בָּרוּךְ אַתָּה, יְיָ, נוֹתֵן הַתּוֹרָה.

*Baruch atah, Adonai Eloheinu, Melech haolam,
asher natan lanu Torat emet, v'chayei olam nata b'tocheinu.
Baruch atah, Adonai, notein haTorah.*

Blessed are You, Adonai our God, Ruler of the universe, who has given us a Torah of truth, implanting within us eternal life.
Blessed are You, Adonai, who gives the Torah.

(The Concluding Prayers can be found on page 106.)

עַרְבִית וְשַׁחֲרִית לְחוֹל

Weekday Evening and Morning Service

Mah Tovu מַה־טֹּבוּ
How Beautiful!

מַה־טֹּבוּ אֹהָלֶיךָ, יַעֲקֹב,
מִשְׁכְּנֹתֶיךָ, יִשְׂרָאֵל!

*Mah tovu ohalecha, Yaakov,
mishk'notecha Yisrael!*

How beautiful are your tents, O Jacob,
your dwelling places, O Israel!

תְּפִלּוֹת הַשַּׁחַר
T'FILOT HASHACHAR
WEEKDAY MORNING SERVICE

מַה־טֹּבוּ
Mah Tovu

אֲשֶׁר יָצַר
Asher Yatzar

אֱלֹהַי נְשָׁמָה
Elohai N'shamah

כָּל בְּשַׂר אִישׁ
Kol B'sar Ish

נִסִּים בְּכָל יוֹם
Nisim B'chol Yom

מִזְמוֹר
Mizmor

תְּפִלּוֹת הַשַּׁחַר
T'FILOT HASHACHAR
WEEKDAY MORNING SERVICE

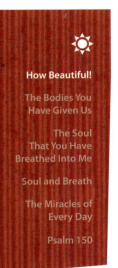

This place is holy.
We make this place holy with our songs.
We make this place holy with our prayers.
We make this place holy with our kindness.

This place is holy.
We make this place holy with our smiles.
We make this place holy with our words.
We make this place holy by simply being here and sharing.

How beautiful is this holy place!
How amazing is this community!

Asher Yatzar אֲשֶׁר יָצַר
The Bodies You Have Given Us

בָּרוּךְ אַתָּה, יְיָ אֱלֹהֵינוּ, מֶלֶךְ הָעוֹלָם,
אֲשֶׁר יָצַר אֶת הָאָדָם בְּחָכְמָה.

*Baruch atah, Adonai Eloheinu, Melech haolam,
asher yatzar et haadam b'chochmah.*

Praise to You, Adonai our God, Ruler of the Universe,
who uses creativity and wisdom to make people.
Our hearts pump, our blood flows and our minds think.
How amazing is this body You have created!

בָּרוּךְ אַתָּה, יְיָ, רוֹפֵא כָל בָּשָׂר וּמַפְלִיא לַעֲשׂוֹת.

Baruch atah, Adonai, rofei chol basar umafli laasot.

Baruch Atah Adonai, who helps us heal the sick
and creates bodies with wonder!

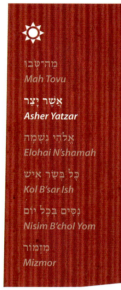

תְּפִלּוֹת הַשַּׁחַר
T'FILOT HASHACHAR
WEEKDAY MORNING SERVICE

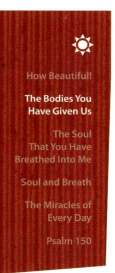

How Beautiful!

The Bodies You Have Given Us

The Soul That You Have Breathed Into Me

Soul and Breath

The Miracles of Every Day

Psalm 150

I sometimes imagine God sitting
on the soft grass in the Garden of Eden
with art supplies scattered about.
Glue and paper,
Clay and crayons,
Colored yarn and colored sand.

God cuts and pastes
Imagines and draws
Pushes and forms the clay into the perfect shape.

I imagine that this is how God made people.
Carefully and creatively, paying attention to every detail,
God formed
Minds that think,
Hearts that pump,
Lungs that breathe,
and bodies that move.

How amazing is this body that You have created for me Adonai!

Baruch atah, Adonai, who helps us heal the sick and creates our bodies with wonder!

Elohai N'shamah אֱלֹהַי נְשָׁמָה
The Soul That You Have Breathed Into Me

אֱלֹהַי, נְשָׁמָה שֶׁנָּתַתָּ בִּי טְהוֹרָה הִיא.

Elohai, n'shamah shenatata bi t'horah hi.

My God, the soul that You have breathed into me is pure and beautiful.

תְּפִלּוֹת הַשַּׁחַר
T'FILOT HASHACHAR
WEEKDAY MORNING SERVICE

מַה־טֹּבוּ
Mah Tovu

אֲשֶׁר יָצַר
Asher Yatzar

אֱלֹהַי נְשָׁמָה
Elohai N'shamah

כָּל בְּשַׂר אִישׁ
Kol B'sar Ish

נִסִּים בְּכָל יוֹם
Nisim B'chol Yom

מִזְמוֹר
Mizmor

תְּפִלּוֹת הַשַּׁחַר
T'FILOT HASHACHAR
WEEKDAY MORNING SERVICE

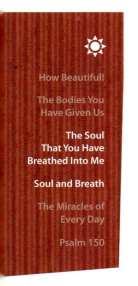

How Beautiful!

The Bodies You Have Given Us

The Soul That You Have Breathed Into Me

Soul and Breath

The Miracles of Every Day

Psalm 150

Kol B'sar Ish כָּל בְּשַׂר אִישׁ
Soul and Breath

בָּרוּךְ אַתָּה, יְיָ, אֲשֶׁר בְּיָדוֹ נֶפֶשׁ כָּל חַי וְרוּחַ כָּל בְּשַׂר אִישׁ.

Baruch atah, Adonai, asher b'yado nefesh kol chai v'ruach kol b'sar ish.

Baruch atah, Adonai, in whose hand is every living soul and the breath of all people.

Nisim B'chol Yom נִסִים בְּכָל יוֹם
The Miracles of Every Day

בָּרוּךְ אַתָּה, יְיָ אֱלֹהֵינוּ, מֶלֶךְ הָעוֹלָם . . .

Baruch atah, Adonai Eloheinu, Melech haolam . . .

תְּפִלּוֹת הַשַּׁחַר
T'FILOT HASHACHAR
WEEKDAY MORNING SERVICE

מַה טֹּבוּ
Mah Tovu

אֲשֶׁר יָצַר
Asher Yatzar

אֱלֹהַי נְשָׁמָה
Elohai N'shamah

כָּל בְּשַׂר אִישׁ
Kol B'sar Ish

נִסִּים בְּכָל יוֹם
Nisim B'chol Yom

מִזְמוֹר
Mizmor

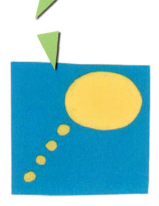
who gives us a mind.

who opens our eyes.

who makes people free.

who strengthens our steps.

who stretches the earth over the waters.

who lifts us up.

70

תְּפִלּוֹת הַשַּׁחַר
T'FILOT HASHACHAR
WEEKDAY MORNING SERVICE

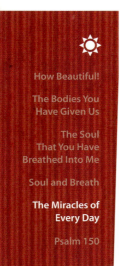

How Beautiful!

The Bodies You Have Given Us

The Soul That You Have Breathed Into Me

Soul and Breath

The Miracles of Every Day

Psalm 150

who makes Israel beautiful.

who makes Israel strong.

who makes us a Jewish family.

who makes us in God's image.

who makes me free.

who wakes us up.

who gives us strength.

who gives us clothes.

71

Mizmor מִזְמוֹר
Psalm 150

הַלְלוּ־יָהּ!

Hal'luyah!

Halleluyah!
Celebrate Life with blasts of the horn,
Celebrate Life with the strum of the harp,
Celebrate Life with tambourine and dance,
Celebrate Life with flute and cymbals.

כֹּל הַנְּשָׁמָה תְּהַלֵּל יָהּ,
הַלְלוּ־יָהּ!

*Kol han'shamah t'haleil Yah,
Hal'luyah!*

Let all that breathes praise God!
Halleluyah!

(The Morning Service continues on page 76 with the Bar'chu.)

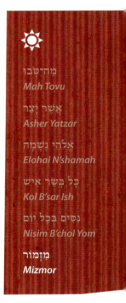

תְּפִלּוֹת הַשַּׁחַר
T'FILOT HASHACHAR
WEEKDAY MORNING SERVICE

מַה טֹּבוּ
Mah Tovu

אֲשֶׁר יָצַר
Asher Yatzar

אֱלֹהַי נְשָׁמָה
Elohai N'shamah

כָּל בְּשַׂר אִישׁ
Kol B'sar Ish

נִסִּים בְּכָל יוֹם
Nisim B'chol Yom

מִזְמוֹר
Mizmor

תְּפִלּוֹת הַשַּׁחַר
T'FILOT HASHACHAR
WEEKDAY MORNING SERVICE

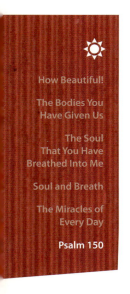

How Beautiful!

The Bodies You Have Given Us

The Soul That You Have Breathed Into Me

Soul and Breath

The Miracles of Every Day

Psalm 150

כֹּל הַנְּשָׁמָה תְּהַלֵּל יָהּ,
הַלְלוּ־יָהּ!

*Kol han'shamah t'haleil Yah,
Hal'luyah!*

Let all that breathes praise God!
Halleluyah!

73

Hineih Mah Tov הִנֵּה מַה־טּוֹב
How Good It Is

תְּפִלּוֹת מַעֲרִיב
T'FILOT MAARIV
WEEKDAY EVENING SERVICE

הִנֵּה מַה־טּוֹב וּמַה־נָּעִים
שֶׁבֶת אַחִים גַּם־יָחַד.

*Hineih mah tov umah na-im
shevet achim gam yachad.*

How good and how pleasant it is
that brothers and sisters dwell together.
(Psalm 133:1)

הִנֵּה מַה־טּוֹב
Hineih Mah Tov

(The Evening Service continues on page 76 with the Bar'chu.)

Bar'chu בָּרְכוּ
Getting Ready to Pray

בָּרְכוּ אֶת יְיָ הַמְבֹרָךְ!
בָּרוּךְ יְיָ הַמְבֹרָךְ
לְעוֹלָם וָעֶד!

Bar'chu et Adonai ham'vorach!
Baruch Adonai ham'vorach
l'olam va-ed!

Praise Adonai to whom praise is due forever!
Praised be Adonai to whom praise is due,
now and forever!

שְׁמַע
וּבִרְכוֹתֶיהָ
SH'MA
UVIRCHOTEHA
THE SH'MA
AND ITS
BLESSINGS

בָּרְכוּ
Bar'chu

מַעֲרִיב עֲרָבִים
Maariv Aravim

יוֹצֵר אוֹר
Yotzeir Or

אַהֲבַת עוֹלָם
Ahavat Olam

אַהֲבָה רַבָּה
Ahavah Rabbah

שְׁמַע
Sh'ma

וְאָהַבְתָּ
V'ahavta

מִי כָמֹכָה
Mi Chamochah

הַשְׁכִּיבֵנוּ
Hashkiveinu

שְׁמַע
וּבִרְכוֹתֶיהָ
SH'MA UVIRCHOTEHA

THE SH'MA AND ITS BLESSINGS

Getting Ready to Pray

Who Creates the Night

Who Creates Light

With Great Love

God's Love

Sh'ma

You Shall Love

Who Is Like You?

Tuck Us In

How do you get ready to pray?
Do you close your eyes,
or do you look around the room
   at everyone who cares about you?

Do you look to the sky and search for God,
or do you look at the earth to see beauty
   in the world around you?

How do you get ready to pray?

77

Maariv Aravim מַעֲרִיב עֲרָבִים
Who Creates the Night

שְׁמַע
וּבִרְכוֹתֶיהָ
SH'MA
UVIRCHOTEHA
THE SH'MA
AND ITS
BLESSINGS

Who paints the world?
Who finds the perfect colors?

The orange of the sun.
The white of the clouds.
The red of the bird's feathers.

Who paints the world?
Who finds the perfect colors?

The silver of the stars.
The gray of the moon.
The yellow of the owl's eyes.

God is the Artist who loves to paint the world.
God is the One who finds the perfect colors.

God is the One who mixes the blue of the day
with the black of the night
and creates the beautiful colors of the evening.

בָּרוּךְ אַתָּה, יְיָ, הַמַּעֲרִיב עֲרָבִים.

Baruch atah, Adonai, hamaariv aravim.

Baruch atah, Adonai, who creates the night.

בָּרְכוּ
Bar'chu

מַעֲרִיב עֲרָבִים
Maariv Aravim

יוֹצֵר אוֹר
Yotzeir Or

אַהֲבַת עוֹלָם
Ahavat Olam

אַהֲבָה רַבָּה
Ahavah Rabbah

שְׁמַע
Sh'ma

וְאָהַבְתָּ
V'ahavta

מִי כָמֹכָה
Mi Chamochah

הַשְׁכִּיבֵנוּ
Hashkiveinu

שְׁמַע
וּבִרְכוֹתֶיהָ
SH'MA
UVIRCHOTEHA
THE SH'MA
AND ITS
BLESSINGS

Yotzeir Or יוֹצֵר אוֹר
Who Creates Light

Getting Ready to Pray
Who Creates the Night
Who Creates Light
With Great Love
God's Love
Sh'ma
You Shall Love
Who Is Like You?
Tuck Us In

The sun rises and the black of the night fades away.
Brilliant oranges, pinks, and yellows fill the sky.
Blessed is the Light of Day.

Animals slowly wake, squinting in the sun,
running, squirming, and sniffing through the grass.
Blessed is the Light of Creation.

People reach out to each other,
helping, supporting, and loving one another.
Blessed is the Light of Peace.

Baruch atah, Adonai:
Blessed is the Light of the World.

בָּרוּךְ אַתָּה, יְיָ, יוֹצֵר הַמְּאוֹרוֹת.

Baruch atah, Adonai, yotzeir ham'orot.

Baruch atah, Adonai, Creator of the lights in the sky.

Ahavat Olam אַהֲבַת עוֹלָם
With Great Love

אַהֲבַת עוֹלָם
בֵּית יִשְׂרָאֵל עַמְּךָ אָהָבְתָּ,
תּוֹרָה וּמִצְוֹת,
חֻקִּים וּמִשְׁפָּטִים, אוֹתָנוּ לִמַּדְתָּ.

*Ahavat olam
beit Yisrael amcha ahavta,
Torah umitzvot,
chukim umishpatim, otanu limadta.*

With great love, God,
You love Your people Israel.
You teach us Torah and mitzvot
and give us laws and rules to live by.

בָּרוּךְ אַתָּה, יְיָ, אוֹהֵב עַמּוֹ יִשְׂרָאֵל.

Baruch atah, Adonai, ohev amo Yisrael.

Baruch atah, Adonai,
who loves Your people Israel.

שְׁמַע
וּבִרְכוֹתֶיהָ
SH'MA
UVIRCHOTEHA
THE SH'MA
AND ITS
BLESSINGS

בָּרְכוּ
Bar'chu

מַעֲרִיב עֲרָבִים
Maariv Aravim

יוֹצֵר אוֹר
Yotzeir Or

אַהֲבַת עוֹלָם
Ahavat Olam

אַהֲבָה רַבָּה
Ahavah Rabbah

שְׁמַע
Sh'ma

וְאָהַבְתָּ
V'ahavta

מִי כָמֹכָה
Mi Chamochah

הַשְׁכִּיבֵנוּ
Hashkiveinu

שְׁמַע וּבְרְכוֹתֶיהָ
SH'MA UVIRCHOTEHA
THE SH'MA AND ITS BLESSINGS

Ahavah Rabbah אַהֲבָה רַבָּה
God's Love

אַהֲבָה רַבָּה אֲהַבְתָּנוּ, יְיָ אֱלֹהֵינוּ,
חֶמְלָה גְדוֹלָה וִיתֵרָה חָמַלְתָּ עָלֵינוּ.

*Ahavah rabbah ahavtanu, Adonai Eloheinu,
chemlah g'dolah viteirah chamalta aleinu.*

You love us, Adonai our God,
like You loved our ancestors.
They trusted You, and You taught them Your Torah.
Teach us Your Torah, too,
and make Your laws a part of our life.

בָּרוּךְ אַתָּה, יְיָ, הַבּוֹחֵר בְּעַמּוֹ יִשְׂרָאֵל בְּאַהֲבָה.

Baruch atah, Adonai, habocheir b'amo Yisrael b'ahavah.

Baruch atah, Adonai,
who chooses Your people Israel with love.

Getting Ready to Pray
Who Creates the Night
Who Creates Light
With Great Love
God's Love
Sh'ma
You Shall Love
Who Is Like You?
Tuck Us In

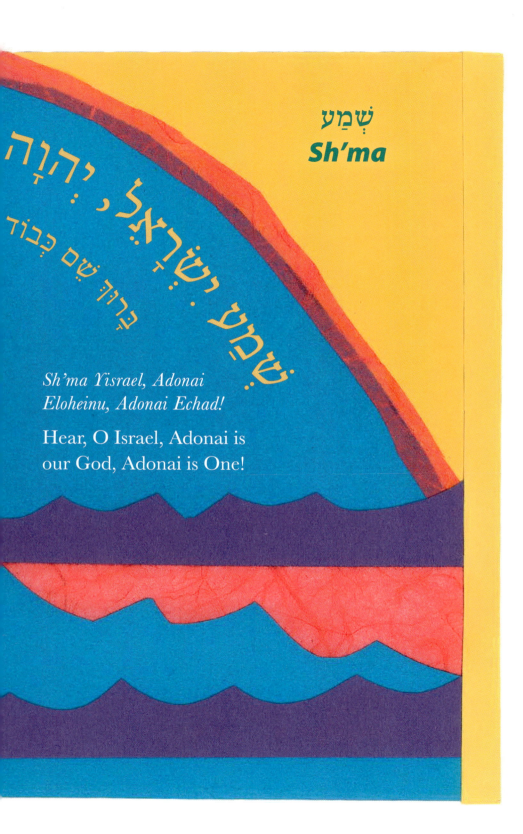

שְׁמַע
Sh'ma

Sh'ma Yisrael, Adonai Eloheinu, Adonai Echad!

Hear, O Israel, Adonai is our God, Adonai is One!

שְׁמַע וּבִרְכוֹתֶיהָ
SH'MA UVIRCHOTEHA
THE SH'MA AND ITS BLESSINGS

בָּרְכוּ
Bar'chu

מַעֲרִיב עֲרָבִים
Maariv Aravim

יוֹצֵר אוֹר
Yotzeir Or

אַהֲבַת עוֹלָם
Ahavat Olam

אַהֲבָה רַבָּה
Ahavah Rabbah

שְׁמַע
Sh'ma

וְאָהַבְתָּ
V'ahavta

מִי כָמֹכָה
Mi Chamochah

הַשְׁכִּיבֵנוּ
Hashkiveinu

שְׁמַע וּבִרְכוֹתֶיהָ
SH'MA UVIRCHOTEHA
THE SH'MA AND ITS BLESSINGS

Getting Ready to Pray
Who Creates the Night
Who Creates Light
With Great Love
God's Love
Sh'ma
You Shall Love
Who Is Like You?
Tuck Us In

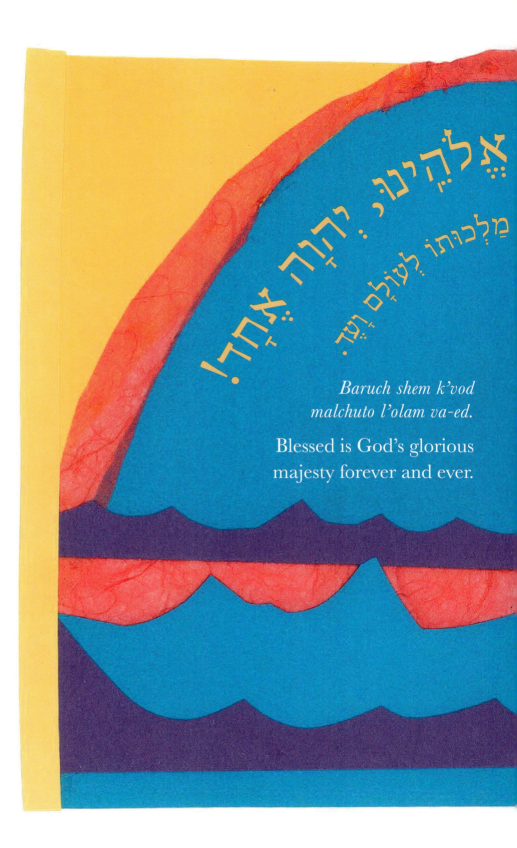

Baruch shem k'vod malchuto l'olam va-ed.
Blessed is God's glorious majesty forever and ever.

V'ahavta וְאָהַבְתָּ
You Shall Love

וְאָהַבְתָּ אֵת יְיָ אֱלֹהֶיךָ,
בְּכָל־לְבָבְךָ, וּבְכָל־נַפְשְׁךָ, וּבְכָל־מְאֹדֶךָ.

V'ahavta eit Adonai Elohecha
b'chol l'vav'cha, uv'chol nafsh'cha, uv'chol m'odecha.

Love Adonai your God with all your heart,
with all your soul, and with all your might.
Take these words that I command today
and keep them in your heart.
Teach them to your children.
Talk about them in your home and on your way,
before you go to sleep and when you wake up.
Put them as a special sign on your hand,
and make them a symbol on your forehead.
Write them on the doorposts of your house
and on your gates.

Remember and follow all of My commandments,
and be a holy people for your God.
I am Adonai, who freed you from slavery in Egypt
to be your God.

יְיָ אֱלֹהֵיכֶם אֱמֶת.

Adonai Eloheichem emet.

I am Adonai your God.

שְׁמַע
וּבְרְכוֹתֶיהָ
SH'MA
UVIRCHOTEHA
THE SH'MA
AND ITS
BLESSINGS

בָּרְכוּ
Bar'chu

מַעֲרִיב עֲרָבִים
Maariv Aravim

יוֹצֵר אוֹר
Yotzeir Or

אַהֲבַת עוֹלָם
Ahavat Olam

אַהֲבָה רַבָּה
Ahavah Rabbah

שְׁמַע
Sh'ma

וְאָהַבְתָּ
V'ahavta

מִי כָמֹכָה
Mi Chamochah

הַשְׁכִּיבֵנוּ
Hashkiveinu

Mi Chamochah מִי כָמֹכָה
Who Is Like You?

מִי־כָמֹכָה בָּאֵלִם, יְיָ!
מִי כָּמֹכָה נֶאְדָּר בַּקֹּדֶשׁ, נוֹרָא תְהִלֹּת, עֹשֵׂה פֶלֶא!

Mi chamochah ba-eilim, Adonai!
Mi kamochah nedar bakodesh, nora t'hilot, oseih fele!

Who is like You, Adonai?
Who is like You, holy and awesome, working wonders?

בָּרוּךְ אַתָּה, יְיָ, גָּאַל יִשְׂרָאֵל.

Baruch atah, Adonai, gaal Yisrael.

Baruch atah, Adonai, who rescues the people Israel.

(The Morning Service continues on page 90 with the T'filah.)

שְׁמַע
וּבִרְכוֹתֶיהָ
SH'MA
UVIRCHOTEHA
THE SH'MA
AND ITS
BLESSINGS

Getting Ready to Pray
Who Creates the Night
Who Creates Light
With Great Love
God's Love
Sh'ma
You Shall Love
Who Is Like You?
Tuck Us In

בָּרוּךְ אַתָּה, יְיָ, גָּאַל יִשְׂרָאֵל.

Baruch atah, Adonai, gaal Yisrael.

Baruch atah, Adonai, who rescues the people Israel.

87

Hashkiveinu הַשְׁכִּיבֵנוּ
Tuck Us In

הַשְׁכִּיבֵנוּ, יְיָ אֱלֹהֵינוּ,
לְשָׁלוֹם, וְהַעֲמִידֵנוּ שׁוֹמְרֵנוּ לְחַיִּים.

*Hashkiveinu, Adonai Eloheinu,
l'shalom, v'haamideinu shom'reinu l'chayim.*

Tuck us into our beds, Adonai our God,
and wake us up feeling strong and healthy.

וּפְרֹשׂ עָלֵינוּ סֻכַּת שְׁלוֹמֶךָ.

Ufros aleinu sukat sh'lomecha.

Spread over us Your blanket of peace.

בָּרוּךְ אַתָּה, יְיָ, הַפּוֹרֵשׂ סֻכַּת שָׁלוֹם עָלֵינוּ וְעַל כָּל
עַמּוֹ יִשְׂרָאֵל וְעַל יְרוּשָׁלָיִם.

*Baruch atah, Adonai, haporeis sukat shalom aleinu v'al kol
amo Yisrael v'al Y'rushalayim.*

Baruch atah, Adonai,
who spreads Your blanket of peace over us,
over all Your people, and over Jerusalem.

שְׁמַע
וּבִרְכוֹתֶיהָ
SH'MA
UVIRCHOTEHA
THE SH'MA
AND ITS
BLESSINGS

בָּרְכוּ
Bar'chu

מַעֲרִיב עֲרָבִים
Maariv Aravim

יוֹצֵר אוֹר
Yotzeir Or

אַהֲבַת עוֹלָם
Ahavat Olam

אַהֲבָה רַבָּה
Ahavah Rabbah

שְׁמַע
Sh'ma

וְאָהַבְתָּ
V'ahavta

מִי כָמֹכָה
Mi Chamochah

הַשְׁכִּיבֵנוּ
Hashkiveinu

שְׁמַע
וּבְרְכוֹתֶיהָ
**SH'MA
UVIRCHOTEHA**

**THE SH'MA
AND ITS
BLESSINGS**

Getting Ready
to Pray

Who Creates
the Night

Who Creates Light

With Great Love

God's Love

Sh'ma

You Shall Love

Who Is Like You?

Tuck Us In

בָּרוּךְ אַתָּה, יְיָ, הַפּוֹרֵשׂ סֻכַּת שָׁלוֹם עָלֵינוּ וְעַל כָּל עַמּוֹ יִשְׂרָאֵל וְעַל יְרוּשָׁלָיִם.

Baruch atah, Adonai, haporeis sukat shalom aleinu v'al kol amo Yisrael v'al Yerushalayim.

Baruch atah, Adonai, who spreads Your blanket of peace over us, over all Your people, and over Jerusalem.

Kavanah כַּוָּנָה
Time to Prepare

תְּפִלָּה
T'FILAH
OUR PRAYER

אֲדֹנָי, שְׂפָתַי תִּפְתָּח,
וּפִי יַגִּיד תְּהִלָּתֶךָ.

*Adonai s'fatai tiftach,
ufi yagid t'hilatecha.*

Adonai, open my mouth
so that I can pray to You with all my heart.

כַּוָּנָה
Kavanah

אָבוֹת וְאִמָּהוֹת
Avot V'Imahot

גְּבוּרוֹת
G'vurot

קְדוּשָׁה
K'dushah

בַּקָּשׁוֹת
Bakashot

עֲבוֹדָה
Avodah

הוֹדָאָה
Hodaah

שָׁלוֹם
Shalom

תְּפִלָּה
T'FILAH
OUR PRAYER

Time to Prepare

Our Fathers and
Our Mothers

God's Power

You Are Holy

Middle Prayers

The Work of Prayer

Praise

Peace

Adonai, Our God, You are the Protector of Abraham and the One who remembers Sarah.
You watched over their children and their children's children.

You were their strength, and with Your help they were able to do great things. They called You the Holy God and knew that You were with them whenever they needed You.

Help me, God, to also know You.
Help me to be strong and brave.
Teach me to be holy.
Help me find the words to thank You, Adonai my God.
Teach me Your peace, and help me be a peacemaker for all the world.

Avot V'Imahot אָבוֹת וְאִמָּהוֹת
Our Fathers and Our Mothers

בָּרוּךְ אַתָּה, יְיָ אֱלֹהֵינוּ
וֵאלֹהֵי אֲבוֹתֵינוּ וְאִמּוֹתֵינוּ,
אֱלֹהֵי אַבְרָהָם, אֱלֹהֵי יִצְחָק, וֵאלֹהֵי יַעֲקֹב,
אֱלֹהֵי שָׂרָה, אֱלֹהֵי רִבְקָה,
אֱלֹהֵי רָחֵל וֵאלֹהֵי לֵאָה.

*Baruch atah, Adonai Eloheinu
veilohei avoteinu v'imoteinu,
Elohei Avraham, Elohei Yitzchak veilohei Yaakov,
Elohei Sarah, Elohei Rivkah,
Elohei Rachel veilohei Leah.*

Blessed are You, Adonai our God
and the God of our fathers and mothers.
You are the God of Abraham,
the God of Isaac, the God of Jacob,
the God of Sarah, the God of Rebecca,
the God of Rachel, and the God of Leah.

תְּפִלָּה
T'FILAH
OUR PRAYER

בָּרוּךְ אַתָּה, יְיָ, מָגֵן אַבְרָהָם וְעֶזְרַת שָׂרָה.

Baruch atah, Adonai, magein Avraham v'ezrat Sarah.

Baruch atah, Adonai,
Abraham's Shield and Sarah's Helper.

תְּפִלָּה
T'FILAH
OUR PRAYER

Time to Prepare
Our Fathers and Our Mothers
God's Power
You Are Holy
Middle Prayers
The Work of Prayer
Praise
Peace

בָּרוּךְ אַתָּה, יְיָ, מָגֵן אַבְרָהָם וְעֶזְרַת שָׂרָה.

Baruch atah, Adonai, magein Avraham v'ezrat Sarah.

Baruch atah, Adonai,
Abraham's Shield and Sarah's Helper.

93

G'vurot גְּבוּרוֹת
God's Power

תְּפִלָּה
T'FILAH
OUR PRAYER

אַתָּה גִּבּוֹר לְעוֹלָם, אֲדֹנָי,
מְחַיֵּה הַכֹּל [מֵתִים] אַתָּה,
רַב לְהוֹשִׁיעַ.

*Atah gibor l'olam, Adonai,
m'chayeih hakol [meitim] atah,
rav l'hoshia.*

You are forever mighty, Adonai. You give life to all.
[Winter] You cause the winds to blow and the rain to fall.
[Summer] Your dew helps the earth to grow.
Who is like You, Source of Power in the world?

בָּרוּךְ אַתָּה, יְיָ, מְחַיֵּה הַכֹּל [הַמֵּתִים].

Baruch atah, Adonai, m'chayeih hakol [hameitim].

Baruch atah, Adonai, who gives life to all.

כַּוָּנָה
Kavanah

אָבוֹת וְאִמָּהוֹת
Avot V'Imahot

גְּבוּרוֹת
G'vurot

קְדֻשָּׁה
K'dushah

בַּקָּשׁוֹת
Bakashot

עֲבוֹדָה
Avodah

הוֹדָאָה
Hodaah

שָׁלוֹם
Shalom

94

בָּרוּךְ אַתָּה, יְיָ, מְחַיֵּה הַכֹּל [הַמֵּתִים].

Baruch atah, Adonai, m'chayeih hakol [hameitim].

Baruch atah, Adonai, who gives life to all.

Evening K'dushah קָדְשָׁה
You Are Holy

תְּפִלָּה
T'FILAH
OUR PRAYER

אַתָּה קָדוֹשׁ וְשִׁמְךָ קָדוֹשׁ
וּקְדוֹשִׁים בְּכָל יוֹם יְהַלְלוּךָ, סֶלָה.

*Atah kadosh v'shimcha kadosh
uk'doshim b'chol yom y'hal'lucha, selah.*

You are holy, God. Your Name is holy.
Those who are holy praise Your Name every day.

בָּרוּךְ אַתָּה, יְיָ, הָאֵל הַקָּדוֹשׁ.

Baruch atah, Adonai, Ha-El HaKadosh.

Baruch atah, Adonai, the Holy God.

Kavanah
Avot V'Imahot
G'vurot
K'dushah
Bakashot
Avodah
Hodaah
Shalom

Morning K'dushah קְדֻשָּׁה
You Are Holy

קָדוֹשׁ, קָדוֹשׁ, קָדוֹשׁ יְיָ צְבָאוֹת,
מְלֹא כָל הָאָרֶץ כְּבוֹדוֹ.

*Kadosh, kadosh, kadosh Adonai Tz'vaot,
m'lo chol haaretz k'vodo.*

Holy, holy, holy is Adonai Tz'vaot!
God's presence fills the whole earth!

Inside me is a holy spark:
a light that shines brightly when I feel proud of myself;
when I feel strong inside;
when I see the beautiful world around me.

Inside each of us is a holy spark:
lights that shine bright when we help one another;
when we are kind to people we don't even know;
when we take care of the world together.

Baruch atah, Adonai, the Holy Spark within us.

בָּרוּךְ אַתָּה, יְיָ, הָאֵל הַקָּדוֹשׁ.

Baruch atah, Adonai, Ha-El HaKadosh.

Baruch atah, Adonai, the Holy God.

Bakashot בָּקָשׁוֹת
Middle Prayers

תְּפִלָּה
T'FILAH
OUR PRAYER

בָּרוּךְ אַתָּה, יְיָ . . .

Baruch atah, Adonai . . .

who gives us knowledge.

who helps us apologize.

כַּוָּנָה
Kavanah

אָבוֹת וְאִמָּהוֹת
Avot V'Imahot

גְּבוּרוֹת
G'vurot

קְדוּשָׁה
K'dushah

בָּקָשׁוֹת
Bakashot

עֲבוֹדָה
Avodah

הוֹדָאָה
Hodaah

שָׁלוֹם
Shalom

who takes care of Israel.

who forgives us.

תְּפִלָּה
T'FILAH
OUR PRAYER

Time to Prepare
Our Fathers and Our Mothers
God's Power
You Are Holy
Middle Prayers
The Work of Prayer
Praise
Peace

who hears our prayers.   who loves truth and justice.   who gives peace to Jerusalem.

who loves kind deeds.   who stops the wicked.   who loves righteousness.

who helps people be free.   who blesses our years.   who heals the sick.

Avodah עֲבוֹדָה
The Work of Prayer

רְצֵה, יְיָ אֱלֹהֵינוּ, בְּעַמְּךָ יִשְׂרָאֵל,
וּתְפִלָּתָם בְּאַהֲבָה תְקַבֵּל.

*R'tzei, Adonai Eloheinu, b'amcha Yisrael,
ut'filatam b'ahavah t'kabeil.*

Be happy, Adonai our God, with Your people Israel,
and accept our prayers with love.

תְּפִלָּה
T'FILAH
OUR PRAYER

כַּוָּנָה
Kavanah

אָבוֹת וְאִמָּהוֹת
Avot V'Imahot

גְּבוּרוֹת
G'vurot

קְדוּשָׁה
K'dushah

בַּקָּשׁוֹת
Bakashot

עֲבוֹדָה
Avodah

הוֹדָאָה
Hodaah

שָׁלוֹם
Shalom

תְּפִלָּה
T'FILAH
OUR PRAYER

Hodaah הוֹדָאָה
Praise

מוֹדִים אֲנַחְנוּ לָךְ.

Modim anachnu lach.

We give thanks to You.

Time to Prepare
Our Fathers and Our Mothers
God's Power
You Are Holy
Middle Prayers
The Work of Prayer
Praise
Peace

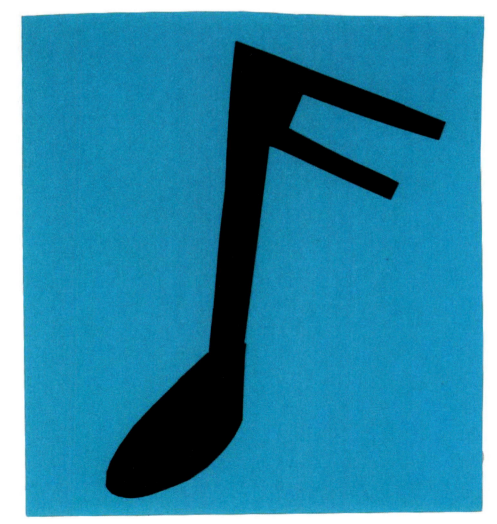

Shalom שָׁלוֹם
Evening Prayer for Peace

תְּפִלָּה
T'FILAH
OUR PRAYER

שָׁלוֹם רָב עַל יִשְׂרָאֵל עַמְּךָ
תָּשִׂים לְעוֹלָם.

*Shalom rav al Yisrael amcha
tasim l'olam.*

Grant peace for Your people Israel
and for all of the world.

(Reading of the Torah can be found on page 56.)
(The Concluding Prayers can be found on page 106.)

כַּוָּנָה
Kavanah

אָבוֹת וְאִמָּהוֹת
Avot V'Imahot

גְּבוּרוֹת
G'vurot

קְדֻשָּׁה
K'dushah

בַּקָּשׁוֹת
Bakashot

עֲבוֹדָה
Avodah

הוֹדָאָה
Hodaah

שָׁלוֹם
Shalom

102

תְּפִלָּה
T'FILAH
OUR PRAYER

Shalom שָׁלוֹם
Morning Prayer for Peace

- Time to Prepare
- Our Fathers and Our Mothers
- God's Power
- You Are Holy
- Middle Prayers
- The Work of Prayer
- Praise
- Peace

שִׂים שָׁלוֹם טוֹבָה וּבְרָכָה,
חֵן וָחֶסֶד וְרַחֲמִים,
עָלֵינוּ וְעַל כָּל יִשְׂרָאֵל עַמֶּךָ.

*Sim shalom tovah uv'rachah,
chein vachesed v'rachamim,
aleinu v'al kol Yisrael amecha.*

Grant peace, goodness, blessing, grace, kindness, and mercy on us and all of Your people, Israel.

(Reading of the Torah can be found on page 56.)
(The Concluding Prayers can be found on page 106.)

סִיּוּם הַתְּפִלָּה

Concluding Prayers

Aleinu עָלֵינוּ
It's Up to Us

סִיּוּם הַתְּפִלָּה
SIYUM
HAT'FILAH
CONCLUDING
PRAYERS

עָלֵינוּ לְשַׁבֵּחַ לַאֲדוֹן הַכֹּל.

Aleinu l'shabei-ach laadon hakol.

Let us now praise the Creator of all,
who made us protectors of the earth
and teachers of the Torah.
You are our God, there is none else.

וַאֲנַחְנוּ כּוֹרְעִים
וּמִשְׁתַּחֲוִים וּמוֹדִים,
לִפְנֵי מֶלֶךְ מַלְכֵי הַמְּלָכִים
הַקָּדוֹשׁ בָּרוּךְ הוּא.

*Vaanachnu kor'im
umishtachavim umodim,
lifnei Melech malchei ham'lachim
HaKadosh Baruch Hu.*

We bow our heads in awe and thanksgiving before You,
the Holy and Blessed One.

עָלֵינוּ
Aleinu

קַדִּישׁ יָתוֹם
Kaddish Yatom

זִכְרוֹנָם לִבְרָכָה
Zichronam
Liv'rachah

Kaddish Yatom קַדִּישׁ יָתוֹם
Mourner's Kaddish

סִיוּם הַתְּפִלָּה
SIYUM HAT'FILAH
CONCLUDING PRAYERS

יִתְגַּדַּל וְיִתְקַדַּשׁ שְׁמֵהּ רַבָּא.
בְּעָלְמָא דִּי בְרָא כִרְעוּתֵהּ, וְיַמְלִיךְ מַלְכוּתֵהּ,
בְּחַיֵּיכוֹן וּבְיוֹמֵיכוֹן וּבְחַיֵּי דְכָל בֵּית יִשְׂרָאֵל,
בַּעֲגָלָא וּבִזְמַן קָרִיב. וְאִמְרוּ: אָמֵן.
יְהֵא שְׁמֵהּ רַבָּא מְבָרַךְ לְעָלַם וּלְעָלְמֵי עָלְמַיָּא.
יִתְבָּרַךְ וְיִשְׁתַּבַּח, וְיִתְפָּאַר וְיִתְרוֹמַם וְיִתְנַשֵּׂא,
וְיִתְהַדָּר וְיִתְעַלֶּה וְיִתְהַלָּל שְׁמֵהּ דְּקֻדְשָׁא בְּרִיךְ הוּא,
לְעֵלָּא מִן כָּל בִּרְכָתָא וְשִׁירָתָא,
תֻּשְׁבְּחָתָא וְנֶחֱמָתָא, דַּאֲמִירָן בְּעָלְמָא. וְאִמְרוּ: אָמֵן.
יְהֵא שְׁלָמָא רַבָּא מִן שְׁמַיָּא,
וְחַיִּים עָלֵינוּ וְעַל כָּל יִשְׂרָאֵל. וְאִמְרוּ: אָמֵן.

☀ ☾

עָלֵינוּ
Aleinu

קַדִּישׁ יָתוֹם
Kaddish Yatom

זִיכְרוֹנָם לִבְרָכָה
Zichronam
Liv'rachah

Yitgadal v'yitkadash sh'mei raba.
B'alma di v'ra chirutei, v'yamlich malchutei,
b'chayeichon uv'yomeichon uv'chayei d'chol beit Yisrael,
baagala uviz'man kariv. V'imru: Amen.
Y'hei sh'mei raba m'varach l'alam ul'almei almaya.
Yitbarach v'yishtabach v'yitpaar v'yitromam v'yitnasei,
v'yit'hadar v'yitaleh v'yit'halal sh'mei d'Kud'sha B'rich Hu,
l'eila min kol birchata v'shirata,
tushb'chata v'nechemata, daamiran b'alma. V'imru: Amen.
Y'hei sh'lama raba min sh'maya,
v'chayim aleinu v'al kol Yisrael. V'imru: Amen.

108

סִיּוּם הַתְּפִלָּה
SIYUM HAT'FILAH
CONCLUDING PRAYERS

It's Up to Us
Mourner's Kaddish
The Blessing of Memory

Exalted and hallowed be God's great name
in the world which God created, according to plan.

May God's majesty be revealed
in the days of our lifetime
and the life of all Israel —
speedily, imminently, to which we say: Amen.

Blessed be God's great name to all eternity.
Blessed, praised, honored, exalted, extolled, glorified,
adored, and lauded
be the name of the Holy Blessed One,
beyond all earthly words and songs of blessing,
praise, and comfort. To which we say: Amen.
May there be abundant peace from heaven, and life,
for us and all Israel.
To which we say: Amen.

עֹשֶׂה שָׁלוֹם בִּמְרוֹמָיו, הוּא יַעֲשֶׂה שָׁלוֹם עָלֵינוּ,
וְעַל כָּל יִשְׂרָאֵל. וְאִמְרוּ: אָמֵן.

Oseh shalom bimromav, Hu yaaseh shalom aleinu,
v'al kol Yisrael. V'imru: Amen.

May the One who creates harmony on high,
bring peace to us and to all Israel.
To which we say: Amen.

Zichronam Liv'rachah זִכְרוֹנָם לִבְרָכָה
The Blessing of Memory

סִיּוּם הַתְּפִלָּה
SIYUM HAT'FILAH
CONCLUDING PRAYERS

We remember people we loved and respect, who are now gone. We think of people we loved, and people who were loving and righteous.

זִכְרוֹנָם לִבְרָכָה.

Zichronam liv'rachah.

May their memories bless us.

עָלֵינוּ
Aleinu

קַדִּיש יָתוֹם
Kaddish Yatom

זִכְרוֹנָם לִבְרָכָה
Zichronam Liv'rachah

Sources

Every effort has been made to ascertain the owners of copyrights for the selections used in this volume and to obtain permission to reprint copyrighted passages. The Central Conference of American Rabbis expresses gratitude for permissions it has received. The Conference will be pleased, in subsequent editions, to correct any inadvertent errors or omissions that may be pointed out.

   3 Bim Bam, Shabbat Shalom, by Nachum Frankel
   4 Shir Chadash, by Julie Silver. Copyright © Julie Silver. Used by permission.
 56 In this scroll is the secret, from *Mishkan T'filah: A Reform Siddur* © 2007 by Central Conference of American Rabbis.
 61 Blessing after the Reading of the Torah, translation from *Mishkan T'filah: A Reform Siddur* © 2007 by Central Conference of American Rabbis.
109 Exalted and hallowed, translation from *Mishkan T'filah: A Reform Siddur* © 2007 by Central Conference of American Rabbis.